The
AWAKENING

of the
date

Sidra Jafri

The
AWAKENING

 **Principles for Finding the Courage to Change your Life**

WATKINS

Sharing Wisdom Since
1893

This book is dedicated to you. I acknowledge your dedication to live an Awakened life.

This edition first published in the UK and USA 2015 by
Watkins, an imprint of Watkins Media Limited
19 Cecil Court, London WC2N 4EZ

enquiries@watkinspublishing.co.uk

10 9 8 7 6 5 4 3 2 1

Designed and typeset by JCS Publishing Services Limited
Printed and bound in Europe

A CIP record for this book is available from the British Library

ISBN: 978-1-78028-797-3

www.watkinspublishing.com

Contents

Acknowledgments

My deepest and heartfelt appreciation to the following:

My parents, Mr and Mrs Jafri – because of them, I am who I am.

My sisters, Bushra and Zara, who stood by me at all times.

My sons, Zain and Hussain, who are wise beyond their ages.

All my teachers, who believed in me before I did.

My ex-husband, Shiraz Zaidi, and his entire family, for all their love and support throughout my journey.

My clients and Awakening participants, who helped to create this book by using the tools and giving me feedback on the best processes to share.

Jo Lal and her team, a Godsend of angels, who showed up at the right time when I was ready to take the Awakening to the world.

Team Awakening, who work around the clock to make Awakening tools accessible around the globe!

Foreword

I have long believed that the best people to guide, teach and heal others through key experiences and traumas are those who have been through similar challenges. The best bereavement counsellors have lost a loved one; a brilliant addiction specialist is one who has had an addiction. The most effective therapists and teachers are often those who have been through a great deal themselves. They have been there and come out the other side.

In my twenties I went on a journey of self-discovery. I needed to because I felt all areas of my life were a mess. I sought out books, teachers and healers. In effect I rebuilt myself. My life changed dramatically. I know first-hand how the right tools can bring dramatic, wonderful change.

I love Sidra's book. She openly shares her traumatic experiences and her journey of self-discovery, including a wealth of case studies, stories and techniques. You do not need to spend years (as I did) searching for the right teachers and techniques; Sidra's research offers you now a wonderful opportunity to clear the past and rebuild your life and your future.

Don't just read this book; work your way through it, make notes, go back and do certain exercises again. That way you will gain so much more.

When I work with people I usually find they are stuck at a certain point or area in their life. Wherever you are right now, however well or not you are doing, there will be something in this book to help create a shift.

I have worked in this field for over 40 years and these days rarely find anything new and fresh, but this book is an exception. Sidra's honest approach and a perfect balance of self-awareness and healing techniques will help you to move forward to a better life.

Anne Jirsch
Author of *Create Your Perfect Future*

INTRODUCTION

Experiencing The Awakening

It is no accident that you picked up this book.

It may be that on some level you already know that it's time for a change. Perhaps you are living a life you didn't choose or a career someone else thought would be a good idea, or are now following a particular path because you thought that's what you were *supposed* to do; what was expected of you. You may also notice how, in certain situations, you sound just like your mother or react exactly like your father, without even thinking about it. Perhaps you have started to notice that some of your behaviours are self-sabotaging or you have acquired habits that you can't seem to shake. Or you are simply aware that your life doesn't feel like yours or have a disquieting sense that your life is not everything it could be.

You may even have started to realize, as I did, that you are living what I call a 'programmed life' – by which I mean a life you didn't consciously choose – but are unsure of how to break free from those binds and reclaim the life you want. Awakening will show you a way to take charge of your life once again, and the first step on the path is to recognize all those beliefs, behaviours and values that don't belong to you – which developed as a result of your upbringing: family traditions, cultural background, education, environment, gender, religious beliefs and other social pressures.

Once you do this, you'll be ready to create new empowering ones – beliefs, behaviours and values that will propel you forward in life. So, to discover the true meaning of Awakening, you must first spy on your life and begin observing your reactions and behaviours. In so doing, you will become aware of all the programs and plug-ins that have been directing your life thus far. However, Awakening is not an event or a set of rules to follow; it is a process that helps you to separate other people's issues from your own and allows you to take full responsibility and charge of your life.

Before my Awakening, I felt disconnected and hollow. It didn't occur to me to question why I wasn't enjoying life. I thought it was just the way things were. I looked around and saw many other people doing the same and simply accepted things as they were. Without realizing it, I was living my life according to others' expectations, opinions, feelings and experiences.

Since Awakening I have lived according to my own truth, instead of being pulled along by an invisible undercurrent. I feel blessed that I understand how to be happy and I want to honour this knowledge by sharing what I call the 'Nine Principles of Awakening' with you, so that you can also have the courage to acknowledge and live with the truth of who you really are. I discovered, as you will too, that life's most challenging lessons are the ones that eventually set you free. You'll discover it is no coincidence that the Awakening has found you when you need it the most, just as it found me.

I look forward to being your guide on your journey of Awakening.

Sidra Jafri

PART I

Awaken To The Nine Principles

'Who looks outside, dreams; who looks inside, awakes.'

Carl Jung

Dying To Live:
Birth Of The Awakening

'The only source of knowledge is experience.'
Albert Einstein

On a warm summer's day in 2002, I woke up in bed and couldn't believe that I was still alive. My head was groggy from the overdose of sleeping pills I'd taken and every muscle in my body felt stiff and raw. I couldn't speak or move, even to open my eyes. Drifting in and out of consciousness, I found myself in a peaceful state of bliss. At that moment, something lit up inside my head and I watched as my entire life story was projected, like a movie in my mind's eye. I viewed scenes from my family life, conversations with friends, arguments and snapshots of moments that defined the choices and decisions I'd made. Watching myself play the starring role in my very own blockbuster, I felt oddly clearheaded and detached. Being an observer with no emotional involvement, I suddenly knew what had been causing me so much pain – 'not wanting to be here' was not new but something I had lived with all my life.

I was born into a middle-class family in Karachi, Pakistan. When my mother was pregnant with me she prayed for a boy. She already had a daughter, but in that culture boys are considered to be an investment in the future while girls are a liability. This feeling of being unwanted later manifested as headaches, nausea and stomach aches. While still only a young girl at school, I displayed neurotic patterns and sought relief in food, self-harming and anything else that would put me at the centre of my parents' world. Of course they did take notice, but not in the way that I'd hoped. By the time I took my first degree I was an emotional wreck. To others, everything appeared to be fine on the surface, but underneath I was struggling.

The same internal struggle continued after I'd married and moved to the UK. Everything should have been good. After all, I had escaped from my domineering parents and was now living a comfortable life with a good husband and, by that time, a beautiful son as well: a dream life for most young women of my background. I couldn't understand why I still felt anxious, lonely, unwell and ill at ease – and it was those feelings that led me to take an overdose. It wasn't the first time that I'd tried to take my own life, but this time I was determined never to feel those same intolerable feelings again . . . only to wake up a few hours later, staring at the same ceiling before losing consciousness. I felt I had done everything I could to feel different and my escape plan had failed. The newfound knowledge that I had *always* felt this way, while helpful, didn't offer a solution. So, when I gained full consciousness, I started praying intensely for help.

Listening for an answer, I suddenly recalled what my schoolteacher had said to me years before. On hearing that I was moving to the UK, he told me how all his students dreamed of such an opportunity and encouraged me to continue my education. He said, 'Leave everything else, but never leave learning.' They say when the student is ready the teacher appears, and those words pulled me back from the brink.

After that day, I realized that no matter how many times I cried or tried to take my own life, there was something bigger than me that was determined I would stay on this earth. I had been given another chance. At that point, I made a decision to continue studying again. I enrolled for a second degree in management and law, and it was there I discovered my passion for human behaviour and my purpose: I wanted to help other people, but I knew I had to find a way to ease my own pain first.

So, I read every book I could find on health, wealth and relationships; and completed diplomas and attended countless workshops on personal development. I loved being a perpetual student and various seminars and courses kept me going in my quest to 'help people'. I was determined to find the root cause of what keeps us stuck and discover a way to rise above our challenges to create the life we truly desire.

Unlocking the mind

I started to understand how our values and beliefs are the sum of the programming within the psyche, and so began to search for a way to rewrite my programs – neuro-linguistic programming (NLP) granted my wish. Developed by Richard Bandler and John Grinder, NLP is a powerful mind tool that makes the connection between the three components that allow us to perceive the world:

Neurology: How we think
Linguistics: How we communicate
Programming: Our beliefs, behaviours and emotions

Training in NLP provided me with a set of tools and techniques that gave me access to that 'central storage system', also known as the mind. Now I understood the mental processes underlying my behaviours and had strategies to replace those programs with more empowering ones. I was still troubled, however, because there was still so much I didn't understand about *why* I had developed all these feelings. Shortly afterwards, however, I started studying Energetic NLP (ENLP) developed by Art Giser and had a breakthrough that was to complete my Awakening.

One evening, while in an ENLP workshop, I felt a massive knot in my stomach. My body seemed to be reacting to the workshop leader's words and, at one point, I felt as though I couldn't breathe, so I asked what was going on. He closed his eyes and, smiling, said: 'Oh, it's your mother's anxiety. You are breaking free from your ancestral patterns . . . 98 percent of who you think you are is not truly who you are, it's other people's energies in your space. Their beliefs, attitudes, stresses, fears all influence our behaviour.' His words opened up a world of questions for me, but finally I knew where to look for the missing piece of my puzzle.

Discovering energies

From that day, I immersed myself in the world of 'energies'. My knowledge of physics was limited, but my hunger for discovering energies was limitless. I explored the concept of 'everything is energy' through Einstein's familiar formula $E=mc^2$, which teaches us that matter and energy are equivalent and we can convert energy into matter. To simplify: everything we perceive – whether it is the air we breathe, our own body, the car we are driving or even the solid brick wall in front of us – is energy. Physics tells us that if we were to break down the structure and form of everything present in this world, we would recognize that underneath it all are the molecules. These molecules are further made up of atoms. Within those atoms are the sub-particles. Once we split these sub-particles, what we observe are electromagnetic waves vibrating at a very high speed or as simply stated 'energy'. So, in reality, the Universe and everything in it is an ocean of vibration. What really distinguishes one form from another is how that energy is coded or put together.

The laws of physics state that energy can neither be created nor destroyed; it is simply converted. So what we experience in our reality is actually a transfer of energy from one system to another. Just like the energy of water when it is heated: first it turns into steam, then it evaporates and forms clouds, which in turn affects the temperature, causing rain, then freezing water that then forms into ice. Water is continually changing form and so changing the structure of its energy. As humans, we rely on our five senses to translate this energetic world into meaningful information. For example: our ears translate the vibration of sound into someone's voice or our touch translates infrared energy as the warmth of our loved one's hands. Just as our eyes decode light and turn it into images.

Humans are highly intelligent beings and we translate this energetic world into meaningful information that we can name, label and categorize as phone, money, wood or laptop, for example. However, we do have sensory limitations and our capabilities are not as developed as other species. Think for a moment about migratory birds that use the earth's magnetic fields to navigate or mosquitoes that are able to detect their prey by using chemical, visual and heat sensors. What we do know is that there is a lot more happening energetically than we are aware of.

Energy also emits frequency and contains information, and this is how we are able to use wireless devices, remote controls and satnavs. In the same way, our body is made up of energetic frequencies and contains information about our lives. It is like a computer that has been programmed by our parents, ancestors, teachers, religions and environment, and it is *that energy* that holds the key to all of our challenges, as well as our successes in life.

Once I understood the characteristics of energy, I could see that my overdoses, self-harming, anger, anxiety, food issues and relationship problems were just another form of energy, created from programs that I had absorbed from my environment. The more I became aware of it, the more I realized I could do something about it. I became certain that I could find a way to access the point of creation of these programs, un-create the outdated, disruptive ones and replace them with the ones that were in alignment with what I truly wanted.

Along with my family, schooling, religion and culture, I now understood how my ancestors had shaped who I was. Each had installed their beliefs or 'programs' of how I should think, perceive and behave in my psyche. For example, my grandfather had committed suicide a long time before I was born and my family didn't speak about it much. Once I started to understand the power of energetic imprints, I realized how I had unwittingly tapped into a dormant memory of my grandfather's death. I began to see that there was a world beyond that of everyday life, where we eat, sleep, work, count calories, brush our teeth and earn money. There is a parallel reality or world that we cannot see. In fact, it is the energetic structure of this unseen world that solidifies the formation of the seen world. Both worlds coexist and are the basis of all our experience. Everything that exists in the seen world has its energetic coding in the unseen world. Once we learn to perceive energetic coding and change it from there, the seen world changes too.

After discovering that one can't exist without the other, I began to balance both realms. I spied on my life, asked my family questions about my ancestors and started working on myself to rewrite those programs. The more I identified with the source of my issues, the easier it became to address them using the tools I was learning. What you don't know you can't solve! My knowledge about myself was increasing and my life was truly changing this time. I felt lighter for the first time in my life and it was liberating.

The journey from waking up in bed that morning *still* alive had taken me nearly four years, but by 2006, armed with two degrees, a diploma in counselling and hypnotherapy, and as a Master NLP Practitioner, trained in ENLP, and a Reiki Master, I was ready to start helping others Awaken too.

Change and growth is inevitable, and the more we align ourselves with this truth the easier our lives will be.

Exploring timelines

Working with clients, I continued to grow and expand my knowledge of energies. I started realizing that we have a central storage system that records everything that happens in our lives. It not only stores information from our present-day life, but also holds the record of events of our past lives and ancestors – they too can affect the programming we run in the present.

Past lives weren't something I even knew about, never mind considered believing in, while I was growing up. The concept of beginning a new life in a new body after death (known as reincarnation) was an alien idea to me. But while my clients were in the state of hypnosis, they were spontaneously recalling events that didn't make sense to them. Using my Access Body Consciousness (ABC) process (which you'll learn on page 37) on those memories, these clients were able to shift the problem and reprogram their behaviours.

AN EYE-OPENING EXPERIENCE

My first encounter with past lives was with a Spanish lady called Bella who came to see me for depression. We used the ABC process to help identify and release the source of her depression and I asked her, 'If the energy of depression could live in your body, where would it live?'

Bella replied, 'Chest.' Then I asked her to imagine that the energy was leaving her body and standing in front of her. I carried on by asking her, 'If it was a person or an event, what would it be?' She started crying and said, 'It looks like a war zone, all the other soldiers are dead and I am the only one alive,' and then she sobbed for ten minutes. When she was calm again, we completed the process.

Afterwards, Bella reported feeling so light, as if she had released that depressed 'fragment' of her, and no longer felt that energy. The process didn't make any sense to either of us, but the result was there.

From then on, I kept an open mind about past lives and evidence of their existence continued to present itself to me. Over time, I came to see how, as the French philosopher Pierre Teilhard de Chardin described it, 'We are spiritual beings having a human experience', because each of our incarnations has an impact on the next.

The other element that has a massive effect on our current life is what happened in the lives of our parents and grandparents. How they lived and their experiences have a huge impact on us. So, the more informed we are about our family's history, the easier it is to discover where the point of creation of our challenges, and even talents, lies. The experience of wars, poverty, death, abortions, miscarriages, murder, suicide, divorce and even physical and mental health in our family line contributes a great deal to our physical, mental, emotional and spiritual make-up in this life.

In my time as an Awakening facilitator, I have seen that every event we experience has its point of creation on these three levels:

Current timeline: The first level consists of information regarding your present lifetime in your body from conception to present.

Eternal timeline: The second level consists of the information of all your past lives contained in the central storage system. Some schools of thought refer to this information as the Akashic Records, which are considered to be an otherworldly archive holding all the information from all of your (and everyone else's) lifetimes.

Ancestral timeline: The third level contains all the information pertaining to the experiences of your parents and of their ancestors. This timeline sometimes holds the key to life-long patterns, which to you seem to have no rhyme or reason.

When you become a spy on your life and start addressing your current challenges, if you find that a particular issue doesn't resolve itself – no matter how many processes you do or how many times you have worked on the issue – then it's time to look beyond your current timeline and start looking into your eternal and ancestral timelines.

The journey of Awakening is multi-faceted and you progress by integrating the experiences from all three levels using the ABC process. The truth is that we are always working on our current timeline, as it is this life that matters the most. The reason I am sharing the information about eternal and ancestral timelines with you is so that you can integrate any unfinished business or missed lessons from your own past lives and release the programs and decisions of your ancestors. In so doing, you will enhance your present life experience and align it with the higher purpose of your soul's journey.

In Awakening we are seeking to recognize our true self so that we can reach our destination.

Birth of the Nine Principles of Awakening

'Awakened' from the conditioning and programming that had been keeping me stuck, I faced another challenge, which I now refer to as an 'identity crisis'. While the change in energy had created a positive transformation in me, I no longer knew who I was and didn't know how I was supposed to live my life. All I understood was that I could now choose to lead a happy and fulfilling existence. But I also wanted to know how to function in my day-to-day life and continue to attract wonderful things into my world.

I was also working with clients who were facing similar identity crises, so over the next six years I developed a method that can be used to not only create an Awakening in us, but also help us to continue to live an awakened life. I have always loved acronyms, so I worked on finding a phrase for each letter of the word AWAKENING. Each phrase is based on the most profound and impactful truths that have shaken my tree, helped me to see the truth of my challenges, empowered me to take charge of the situation and created a long-term solution. Those phrases were:

A Ask quality questions
W Work on you
A Awareness is the key
K Knowing versus owning
E Energy is everything
N No judgment
I It takes one to see one
N Nothing is missing
G Growth is inevitable

Little did I know that those key phrases would become the Nine Principles of Awakening, which have now helped thousands of other people, from all walks of life, to wake up and live Awakened lives. Those people have seen real and tangible results when they applied the principles to their day-to-day lives, and these are the same tools and techniques I will be sharing with you in this book. Once you apply them and make them part of your life, I know they will work for you too. Every time we face a challenge, we can refer to the Nine Principles of Awakening and see which one requires attention. Observing your three timelines and then working to transform the energy where you are stuck using the Nine Principles, you'll discover how to:

- make peace with your past
- live fully in the present
- discover your purpose
- empower yourself to create the life and future that you truly deserve.

If I could do anything in the world, absolutely anything, I would still do this work because I know it has the power to change your life as much as it did mine – and continues to do so every day. Consider this book a toolbox for building the ultimate life that you desire.

CHAPTER ONE

Awakening From A Programmed Life

'Nothing has such power to broaden the mind as the ability to investigate systematically and truly all that comes under thy observation in life.'

Marcus Aurelius

Visualize for a moment William Shakespeare's idea of 'All the world's a stage, and all the men and women merely players.' In fact, we're not just the 'players', we're also the scriptwriters, directors and producers of our own play called 'life'. However, unaware of this, how often do we let our parents, teachers, peers, religious beliefs or lack of them and our environment write our script and direct our play? Sometimes we even act out our parents' dreams and programming not knowing that it is not our own.

My first degree was my father's dream of 'becoming an accountant', while my marriage was a result of witnessing my parents' interaction in their relationship. If you are having relationship issues, where you keep attracting the same type of situation or partner, the chances are that you're enacting your parents' programming – perhaps they split up when you were young or had a challenging relationship. Or if you find yourself chasing a certain dream, chances are that you picked up the idea of that dream from one of the above-mentioned sources.

Of course the reverse is also true, and we also pick up positive programming as we are growing up, which serves us well and is the reason why we brush our teeth twice a day, work hard at our jobs or have other life-affirming behaviours – and I remain truly grateful for everything that my parents did for me. So, in observing your life, it is important to acknowledge all your positive values, beliefs and behaviours while seeking to awaken from anything that is keeping you stuck and not aligned with the life you truly want.

Signs of Awakening

Awakening interacts with us on four levels (physical, mental, emotional and spiritual) and here follow some of the common signs that you have already begun to awaken:

> **Physically:** You may experience aches and pains that seem to appear out of nowhere and/or have ailments that don't respond to conventional medicine.
>
> **Mentally:** You may have negative thoughts, find it difficult to concentrate and struggle to enjoy activities and hobbies that you once loved.
>
> **Emotionally:** You may experience mood swings and feel overwhelmed with emotion. You may also find it difficult to relate to colleagues, friends or your partner out of fear of getting close to people.
>
> **Spiritually:** You may experience a feeling of emptiness and question your purpose in life.

You can go through Awakening on more than one level at a time, or even all four simultaneously. However to transform the energy of your programming (energetic imprints, which you'll learn to access on page 27), it is important first to understand how the mind really works and that it operates on three levels:

Conscious: The part of your mind that is aware right now, and is responsible for paying attention and focusing.

Subconscious: This is like the software of a computer and is where all your programming is stored. It dictates where you live, how much money you earn, what type of work you do, even the sort of person you are attracted to.

Superconscious: While the conscious and subconscious aspects of your mind are closely aligned with your physical body, the superconscious is connected with the unseen realm. It exists at a level extending beyond what our five senses can perceive and exists in our energetic thought forms. When we are accessing our eternal and ancestral timelines we are connected to this part of our mind.

You might find it easier to think of your conscious mind as the computer (hardware) while the subconscious mind is the software (programming), which runs your conscious mind, the computer, and is closely aligned to your physical body. The third part, your superconscious mind, is the Internet and connected with the energetic realm. It exists at a level extending beyond the space–time continuum and has the ability to link to every other mind on the planet.

In order to get in touch with our subconscious and super-conscious, we need to be able to bypass the conscious brain and the fastest way to do this is by inducing a meditative or trance state. Many people are wary about 'hypnosis' and think it means someone else (the hypnotist) having control of their mind, but this is not the case – the participant is always in control.

The truth is that we actually go in and out of these trances all the time, usually when we are doing something familiar, such as driving our usual route to work, brushing our teeth or washing the dishes. They can also occur when we are doing something mentally creative – such as writing or playing music; or emotional – such as making love; or spiritual – praying or meditating; or physical – running or walking. Afterwards, we can't actually remember doing the act, but that's because we were no longer using our conscious brains. We were in the moment and in a dream-like state where we were connected to our innermost thoughts and feeling (or energy). Some people talk about this as being 'in the flow', and inducing a hypnotic state is simply a way of inducing that flow-like state at will, so that we can speak to the subconscious and superconscious parts of the brain and make positive changes to our energy.

Discovering your programs

When I first started learning NLP and ENLP, I worked intensely on my own development so that, in time, I could help others out of their stuck-ness and find their energy. In that time I learned that it is possible to see all our difficult issues as true gifts, rather than problems or misfortune. This might sound strange, but our trials and tribulations allow us to look beyond our current understanding of life and urge us to explore possibilities we didn't think existed before. We learn and evolve through our difficulties as we embark on a quest for meaning. The following describes how this process works.

During my first session, I focused on the deep sadness that I had felt all my life and traced the energy back to when it was imprinted – which was all the way to the time when I was born. I could sense my mother's disappointment and relived that same sadness as a newborn. Then I worked on transforming the energy of that imprint by communicating to my infant self. Using the power of imagination, I cradled myself as a newborn and told her that she was loved and wanted – I visualized the sadness leaving my baby self and love entering.

We can do this type of work on ourselves because as adults we are able to perceive situations differently and therefore transform how the event affected us – which in turn changes our present experience of who we are.

After that session, I felt different and, for the first time, truly loved, which immediately changed how I related to life. Being able to accept and appreciate myself transformed my relationships, which in turn helped my health and I started to experience a sense of wellbeing and health.

Each session, I picked a past event that had hurt me or upset me, induced a trance-like state by relaxing and focusing on my breath and then worked on identifying where my energy was coming from and what it was teaching me. Once I was able to visualize all my emotions as energy in motion I could trace them back to the point of creation and then transform the energy into something more life-giving, creative and aligned with my heart's desires. For example, I discovered that the energy of fear surrounded how I felt about money and so I worked on transforming that emotion into one of excitement, and so my finances started improving.

Becoming aware

So your first step on your journey of Awakening is to become aware of any issues that require attention. Ask yourself where you might be following yourself blindly; where your habits, traditions and ideas of yourself may need updating or shifting. Start an Awakening journal and write your observations down in as much detail as possible. Consider where the issue might have started, how it manifests in your life and how it affects you on the four levels: physical, mental, emotional, spiritual. If you are experiencing any signs of Awakening (listed on page 18), then you are already beginning to become aware of the scripts (programming) you have been running in your life from your current timeline, or carried forward from your eternal timeline, or may have been affecting your family for centuries (ancestral timeline). This work will help clarify how that energy is affecting your life.

Don't worry if you begin to question everything. We don't tend to look for the answer until something stops working, so see this questioning as taking action before things go wrong.

The source of our values, beliefs and behaviours

After spending many years helping people, I have found that whatever issue you are currently facing, it is unlikely to be a new problem. It is more likely that the issue you are dealing with in adulthood is an unresolved problem that happened during your formative childhood years. The problem is that many of us spend our lives believing what our environment taught us to believe. Our first instinct when we are born is to survive and in order to survive we take on the point of view of everyone around us. These points of view create our 'beliefs' and, like the monks in the following story who thought tying the cat was a holy practice, this is also how most traditions are formed.

THE MONASTERY'S CAT

The monks of one particular monastery in Tibet were renowned for their spiritual practice, spending their days absorbed in profound meditation. But one day a cat stalked into the monastery grounds and interrupted the monks' practice with its infernal screeching. This enraged the head monk so much that he ordered his monks to trap the cat and tie it to the banyan tree until nightfall, the time when the monks would end their meditation. Furthermore, he ruled that the cat should be tied to the tree in the same way every day, to prevent such disruption ever happening again. And so tying the cat to the banyan tree became part of the monks' habitual practice. When the head monk came to the end of his life, his replacement continued all the monastery's customs, not omitting the practice of catching and tying up the cat every day. When the cat died, however, no one in the monastery knew what to do. How could they continue their usual daily practice without the cat? Eventually, after much thought, everyone agreed that a new cat must be purchased, so that the monks could catch it and tie it to the banyan tree before they began their meditation each day.

In the same way, most people take beliefs to be something that appears to be absolutely true for them. It is their understanding of the world. For example, if I believe that apples are good for me, then it must be due to evidence or experience that has created that belief; it has become a truth. Somewhere in my mind I will have enough resources to believe this is the case. Some of these beliefs are helpful, such as the one that fruit and vegetables are good for us – due to that belief we eat a healthy diet. However, others are not. For example, we might grow up believing that we always fail, that we are unlucky or that we are not good enough (because we were often told this as a child), or that eating ice cream will make the hurt go away, or that relationships always end in heartbreak.

In adulthood, our beliefs can manifest as all sorts of issues, including low self-esteem, destructive relationships and bad habits, because the programmed voice in our head keeps telling us, for example, 'I am not good enough' or

'I am unlucky' or 'This food will make me feel better' or 'I will get hurt if I get too close to them.' Our beliefs are personal to us and the list of possible beliefs is endless but they have one thing in common: our beliefs are powerful because they are always backed up by evidence.

All the beliefs that parents hold about the world are automatically installed in their child's memory at conception, along with their biological genes and cellular make-up, and these affect what the child believes about the world. This may sound unbelievable, but there have been many cases where children have been separated from their natural parents at birth, but have grown up with similar traits due to nature not nurture. Take, for example, the true story told by Elyse Schein and Paula Bernstein in *Identical Strangers* of twins who were separated at birth and yet developed strikingly similar behaviours. Epigenetics, the study of inherited traits and behaviours, is currently one of the hottest topics in psychology, and while more research is needed, we do know that our genetics aren't just limited to physical traits but can affect our behaviours (which are due to our beliefs) at a cellular level.

So when the child is born those inherited beliefs are strengthened by the parents' behaviours and practices, and because the child has some common beliefs with the parents it's more than likely they will act the same way and attract similar situations as they grow into adulthood. Due to their beliefs they may find that they are having similar experiences as their parents, and this is why it's not uncommon to find that we often make the same mistakes as our parents.

So our beliefs create what we hold to be important, and we usually define these beliefs as our 'values'. Our values are the system that drives our actions and behaviours; they are a road map of how we think we should behave and what our lives should reflect and look like. For example:

Belief: 'I must work hard to earn a living.'

Value: 'I must work hard for my money, even if it's in a job I don't enjoy', 'laziness is bad', 'work is more important than family and friends', 'money is really important', etc.

Behaviour: Mentally – this may manifest as feeling constantly stressed and under pressure, and an inability to switch off from work; emotionally – relationships with family and friends may be poor because work takes priority over others and personal needs for rest and enjoyment; spiritually – feelings of isolation might pervade as commerce rules rather spiritual nourishment; physically – working too much might result in not exercising and eating a poor diet, and so minor or major health issues ensue from poor lifestyle habits and too much stress.

The energy of this one belief demonstrates how it can affect the whole of our life and result in us assuming a life that we didn't choose. Awakening is about examining and transforming the energy of our beliefs so that they create positive and life-affirming values that result in behavioural changes, which in turn impact life physically, mentally, emotionally and spiritually.

Storing our beliefs (programs)

Our memories also form part of our beliefs and values system, together with the decisions and promises we made to ourselves, and determine the type of life that we are currently living. For example, if you fell into a paddling pool when you were three years old and struggled to get out, then you may have decided that water is deadly. You never learned to swim, you hate going on boats and aren't even that keen on the beach. The deal you made was a logical one at the time and its aim was to protect you from further harm, but the water you fell into as a child would barely come above your ankle now that you are an adult. Yet the experience is still very real to you on some level.

Mainstream science tells us that the brain alone is responsible for holding our memories. However, new research is beginning to change this old paradigm. Take the example of David Waters. According to a story published by the *Daily Mail* in 2009, he received a heart transplant from 18-year-old Kaden Delaney, who was left brain-dead after a car crash. After the transplant David found that he developed a craving for a particular brand of burger-flavoured snacks, and when he spoke to Kaden's family he discovered that Kaden used to eat these snacks daily. This is one of many other examples where transplant recipients suddenly take on the characteristics of the donor, but how is this possible?

Caroline Myss, best-selling author of *Anatomy of the Spirit*, says, 'our biography becomes our biology'. She describes how the body, not just the brain, has the ability to store information such as memories, sensations, emotions, personality and even trauma in the neurons of its cells. This is often referred to as 'cellular memory' and is a compilation of our entire life. As the brain and the organs are constantly communicating, each cell has access to this entire information.

> Think of your body as a computer and each cell within it as a separate RAM containing all the files.

Our memories are not bound by time, either, because this is not a concept that the mind understands, which is why traumatic events can still feel very new and raw many years later. In its most extreme form, when the event or circumstances are deeply traumatizing, such as rape or being in military conflict, this can result in disorders such as post-traumatic stress disorder (PTSD). The mind simply views the images irrespective of whether they occurred in the present or years before and has no way of distinguishing what is real or unreal in the present moment. Each memory we access is remembered as if we were living it now. For example, when we feel low or depressed after an uneventful day, it is not usually due to the day's events but because, in some way, these have triggered a memory from the past and we relive that event or set of circumstances over and over again in our present. As when we feel anxious about our future, the body reacts as if imagined events are currently taking place, and we may even experience the flight-or-fight response and experience an adrenalin rush, even when nothing is actually happening externally in that moment.

Energetic imprints and timelines

In the same way, many people come to me with relationship issues. Often their problem occurred in their current timeline when they were perhaps six or seven years old. They may, for example, have witnessed their parents fighting and arguing, and promised themselves that they would avoid the same pain by not getting married. As time goes on, they consciously forget all about that experience and start looking for their perfect partner, but as soon as things start to go well and marriage is on the cards they get 'cold feet' and everything breaks down. Why? Because they are still living the promise they made to a younger version of themselves.

ARMING AGAINST LOSS
Brenda came to see me because she wanted to resolve a long-standing weight issue. She had been trying for years to shift the extra pounds by trying every diet available, but always ending up eating foods that were bad for her. I used a guided meditation to help

her discover the source of her beliefs about food. It turned out that her father's death when she was six years old left her feeling very vulnerable and small. Gaining weight then made her feel more protected and bigger, and she carried that belief into adulthood and discovered 'when I comfort eat, I feel the love from my father'. Once we were able to transform this belief about food, Brenda found that she was able to maintain her diet without the self-sabotaging belief that the food made her feel loved and protected her.

Sometimes the point of creation of a belief can be traced to the eternal or ancestral timelines, even though the challenge we might be facing is showing up in our current timeline. The truth is that every event we experience is multi-faceted and it's important to keep that in mind when you start to integrate those parts of you that have been ignored for so long. Accessing timelines using the ABC process (which you'll learn on page 37) can also reveal events and circumstances that have been holding you back, as the next case study demonstrates.

CHILDHOOD VOWS

Amanda was in love with a man who abused her, but she couldn't break free from the relationship no matter how hard she tried. After seven years of misery, she came to a live Awakening event and we carried out a process to find out when she had created this issue. She knew little about her mother or maternal family, but working on her ancestral timeline she discovered to her astonishment that her mother and her grandmother had been in abusive relationships too. Going deeper, she recalled an event where her dad had come home drunk and beaten her mother. She was 12 and suddenly remembered feeling very scared for her mother. Desperately wanting her to feel better she made a vow to herself that she would have a bad relationship too in an effort to try and make her mother feel better. This is not uncommon, as children often believe that taking on the same pain will help their parent heal. Once Amanda had identified what had been holding her back, she was able to acknowledge it, heal it and then let it go.

The vows and pacts made in our eternal timeline also have an impact on our current life. I believe that in the soul plane (the place we return to before incarnating back on earth), we exist as a soul of pure spiritual energy with no ego or earthly ties. Without the burden of emotional attachment, we are able to see what we need to learn from each lifetime, or what we can do to help teach others, in order to evolve spiritually. Other souls – people we will meet on earth – make pacts or agreements with us, and we with them, to help create experiences that will allow us to absorb the knowledge and grow spiritually.

For example, if there is someone in your life right now who has wronged, abused or hurt you, or someone you are unable to let go of, imagine if you could discover why you chose to experience all the pain (or the joys) of that relationship before you were born. I believe that's exactly what happened. You made the decision to meet that person so that you could mutually have an experience together from which you both would learn. The thing that surrounds the truth of your relationship is what is called the 'Veil of Amnesia', between the conscious and superconscious mind.

The Veil plays an essential part in making sure we go through the spectrum of emotions required for an enriched and fulfilling experience that is necessary for our evolutionary journey. It allows us to experience all of life's ups and downs so that we can integrate them into our psyche.

Explore the power of this idea by imagining for a moment that you are a soul planning your next incarnation on earth. You decide to experience the lesson of self-empowerment. In order to learn the lesson, you agree a contract with another soul who will become your partner and you will have children together. Together you decide that when your children are three and six, he will fall in love with another woman and abandon you. After going through the pain, you will learn the lesson of self-empowerment by having to take responsibility for your children alongside many other growth lessons about courage, forgiveness and not judging.

If there were no Veil of Amnesia, the year your kids turned three and six, you would start searching for the 'other woman' your partner is going to leave you for, and ask, 'Isn't this the time you were supposed to leave me?' This would obviously dilute the shock and emotional impact of the lesson you have chosen to learn. You would not appreciate life's lessons if you already knew you were 'going home' at the end of it. The very point of each life on this planet, the earth plane, is to learn and evolve through our emotional experiences and recognize the higher purpose of our relationships. We may not remember the agreements made in the soul plane consciously, so when these spiritual beings show up as family members, friends, lovers or even enemies, they offer our biggest challenges wrapped in the Veil of Amnesia, so that we can work through our lessons as a result of those relationships. Sometimes the most loving beings in your life are also the ones who agreed in the soul plane to teach you the most painful lessons on the earth plane.

It is also true that not everyone you meet in your life has made an agreement with you in the soul plane. On the other hand, you'll probably instinctively know some of the people you encountered there. Often these are people you have a strong bond with, and you may intuitively know that you have met them before. They may also be people who have passed away that had an impact on your life or people who will become an important part of your future, that are as yet unfamiliar to you.

This is exactly what Awakening is about in spiritual terms – lifting the Veil of Amnesia to see the truth of your experiences. Recognizing the lesson in any challenging situation is one of the keys to living an Awakened life. And in the next chapter you will learn how to start burning the Veil and seeing the purpose of your incarnation.

CHAPTER TWO

Beginning Your Inner Journey

'My different personalities leave me in peace now.'
Anna Freud

My inner journeys have led me to profound discoveries of different aspects of myself of which I was previously totally unaware. These aspects, or parts, often had a discrete persona and were playing different roles in my life. Looking at your own life you will see this is true too, because we all play different roles in different situations. For example, there's a professional work-oriented 'you' that is different to the fun-loving, sociable 'you' or the addictive, defensive or scared 'you'.

In traditional psychotherapy it has been long understood that when we experience a trauma a 'part' of us splits off and creates a personality of its own. Many mainstream therapies include 'part works', and this concept isn't new. In traditional counselling, for example, these 'parts' of our personalities are often described as 'inner children'.

This part secretly relives the memory over and over again because the conflict is unresolved. For example, anyone who has experienced mental or physical abuse or a shocking event, such as a car accident, knows that the memory gets played over and over again, whether they are conscious of it or not. What's more, there will often be physical aspects to the memory, such as a certain smell or sound. The part, or 'fragment' as I call it, that splits off at the time of the event relives that situation with the same mindset or energy that was created at the time. This means the memory can become active if we are faced with a situation that even slightly resembles the original experience and the 'fragment' is triggered to respond to the new event with the same mindset or energy, which is stored in the psyche.

As I described in the previous chapter (see page 19), our subconscious has no concept of time and is unable to understand that what was hurtful in the past is no longer valid. Traumatic and stressful life experiences continue to affect us long after the event because we still have a relationship with them, so they keep repeating. In essence, the problem is not with us, it's with that fragment of us that got left behind and now requires attention. It was unloved, undesired or there was something wrong with it. Your psyche was not able to deal with the pain at the time, so instead it developed a survival strategy, which was entirely appropriate for a young child or teen but isn't working for you as an adult.

Anxiety, panic attacks, heart palpitations and angry episodes are all classic signs that our stuck memories are bringing their energy to our present-day life. The reason we feel the physical response to these events is because these memories have a home in our body due to the fifth principle: Energy Is Everything. Once you understand that it's your frozen fragment that requires attention and not you that need fixing, you can begin to heal yourself. What's more, what you are dealing with is just a younger version of you that is keen to be brought gently into the present, so that it can finally be free of reliving something that happened in the past.

Taking an inner journey requires us to go inside ourselves and collect all those disconnected 'fragments' and release them by healing them with love.

I have many clients who tell me that, logically, they know how they ought to behave when dealing with a stressful situation.

Yet, when faced with the particular set of circumstances that trigger them, or while interacting with a stranger or a new person, they react in a way that feels as though someone else has taken over, and they often say 'You've got to believe me, I wasn't myself: that wasn't me! I don't know what came over me.' And then ask, 'Why do I keep doing that?'

The good news is that when you recognize it's not you but just a fragment of who you are, then it becomes much easier to control. Once you integrate the isolated fragment you can acknowledge and appreciate the aspect of you that has been ignored for so long. It is a gift from the dark that you can transform into a vibrant, multi-dimensional and fully present side of you.

Understanding your triggers

Each fragment contains all the information about the traumatic event. The details about the event are numbed in our conscious mind and it may feel as though it never happened. Or we may have memories about it but we, or someone else, decided that we had gotten over it, that we were a grown-up and therefore it need not affect us. This is a protection mechanism created by your subconscious mind so that you can continue living a functional life and are not overwhelmed by the emotions created by the event. The key to remember is that all the information is complete and accounted for; it doesn't go away just because you don't remember it. It lives on in your subconscious and dictates your future responses to new people, situations and events.

Each time the experience is repeated, that fragment is reactivated in the subconscious, adding another layer, another imprint, to the original event. These build up slowly and steadily and eventually solidify. They first affect the more subtle mental, emotional and spiritual bodies, but eventually take a toll on the physical body, too. This is the time when your body starts to send clear messages by giving you aches and pains so that you starting paying attention! Anything that acts to remind you of the earliest memory of the event can be viewed as a trigger. A look, word, sound, smell, taste, colour or sometimes it could even be a certain person who might remind you of that event. The trigger alerts your subconscious mind, which tunes you back, almost immediately, into the original event. Suddenly you are flooded with the energy of the memory, although you might not even be conscious of it. The signs of Awakening (see page 18), whether they are physical, mental, emotional or spiritual, are alerts from our body, asking us to integrate the isolated fragments of our personality.

ISADORA'S STORY

Isadora was diagnosed with depression when she was two years old and at 36 she rarely felt joyful or laughed. Using guided meditation we were able to 'access her program' of depression. I asked her to imagine that she was floating over a path that represented her timeline going into her past, all the way back to when she was in her mother's womb and see herself as an embryo. She started sensing what was happening around her at that time and was able to feel that her mother was depressed. Isadora was her mother's sixth pregnancy and her mother felt conflicted about whether or not to terminate the pregnancy. Isadora communicated her love and appreciation to that fragment and told that much younger version of herself that she was no longer in the womb and it was safe for her to let go of this depression.

By the time Isadora came for her next session, she had undergone a complete 180-degree turnaround and was beaming. The transformation and the shift in her physiology came from integrating her prenatal memory and updating her cellular memory, which previously held her mother's depression.

Reintegrating the fragments

I developed the Access Body Consciousness (ABC) process by synthesizing the techniques I learned on my own journey since 1999. My encounters with thousands of clients since 2006 have enabled me to refine the process into one omnipotent tool that can be used to address all manner of issues, from clinical depression or chronic back pain to working on fears or addressing procrastination. I recommend using the ABC process throughout the Nine Principles of Awakening to help you integrate all those fragments that you have left in time and space, and replace them with new empowering decisions that will lead to an Awakened life

Access Body Consciousness (ABC) process

Consciously integrating fragments of yourself will help you rise above blame, make your own choices and take charge of your own actions. Ultimately, learning to use this five-step technique, and then practising it regularly, will help you to experience unconditional love, which dissolves all separation.

Find a place where you can relax and won't be disturbed. Make yourself comfortable, perhaps by lying down and covering yourself up with a blanket. Now close your eyes. Take a few deep, cleansing breaths and feel centred in your body. Enjoy the feeling of peace as you just focus on your inward and outward breaths for as long as it takes for you to become present in this moment.

1 Identification
Identify where the 'fragmented' part resides in your body by asking a quality question:

- If I could sense the part of me that is scared/angry/ hurt/anxious, where in my body would it live?

Now follow your physical intuition, for example you might have a sensation in your gut or feel discomfort in a particular place; this is where the fragment resides. Once you have identified where that fragment is situated, focus all your attention and awareness on that area.

Now rate its intensity between 0–10 with 10 being its strongest and 0 being nothing there at all. The reason we give it a number is so we can gauge the effect of the process. What we can measure we can improve.

2 Acceptance
Every fragment contains a promise, a vow or a decision that requires attention and acceptance. After identifying what that is, the next step is to accept the message that has been stored for you. To accept the message ask the following questions:

- If this fragment could speak to me, what would it say?
- Does it have a man's voice or a woman's voice?
- If that fragment had a colour, what colour would it be?

- If that fragment of me had a age, what age would it be?

This step is often the most profound because many people have never communicated with any of their fragments before. You may find doubts and resistance kick in at this step. The best way to overcome resistance is to use your imagination. For example, if you ask yourself the above questions and the answer comes, 'I don't know', then keep going by saying, 'If I did know?' or 'If I could make it up, what would it be?' In this way, we are able to bypass the conscious mind's filter of judgment and access the subconscious.

3 Release
Now, using your thoughts, imagine that energy is spiralling out of your body, taking all the pain with it. That energy is now standing in front of you.

To dissolve the energy say, 'I love you, I am sorry. Please forgive me. I forgive you. I release any promises or decisions that I made to you or to myself at that time. We are both free. Thank you.'

By saying this statement you are releasing all the negative energy surrounding that part and it is now gone from your body.

4 Replace
Because nature always fills the void, once your block has been reduced or totally eliminated it is very important to replace the space that has been left with an emotion that better serves you. What feeling would you like to replace that space with? It could be love, peace, compassion, faith, happiness or any other feeling you like.

Give the feeling a colour, then imagine a big ball of energy coloured with that emotion in your mind's eye . . . Now breathe the feeling in a few times to draw it in and fill the space where the original fragment lived. When you breathe out, imagine breathing out any resistance that you are feeling.

5 Celebrate

Celebration is the last step and the most important of all. It helps to integrate the new energy with ease, grace and joy to make sure you end on a high note.

Tailor your words to suit your purpose but, for example, you might say: 'I love, honour and acknowledge myself for being open and receptive to change. I am now celebrating my success by [*insert an action that you associate with success*].'

Now it is time to do something that cements the feeling, and gives you a feeling of celebration and completion. It might be anything from having a relaxing cup of tea and reading a book to booking a vacation. By celebrating in some way you are affirming that it is safe for you to have released that part of you and replace it with the new feeling.

Many of us make childhood decisions, promises or pacts, which impact on all aspects of our lives as adults. The clues to these unspoken promises and decision are in our speech. Sentences like: 'I will never . . .' or ' I will always . . .' indicate an unspoken promise within.

When you find the courage to push past the fear of change using the ABC process given above, you will understand some aspects of your life on a whole new level. You might still not know why certain things are happening, but you will feel comfortable with that. Understanding your life from an Awakened point of view gives you the recognition that you are not alone in this journey; we are all together. You will learn how to clear blocks and energetic undercurrents using the ABC process so that you can experience abundance in health, wealth and relationships.

Awakening is not an event, it is a way of being.

Warning: Change ahead!

Thousands of people join me at my Awakening events in the hope of changing their relationships, getting better jobs or improving their health. I always say to them, 'Be careful what you wish for because it will come true.' So many times we think we desire particular things in life but the reality is that we might not be willing to sacrifice other activities to attain those goals. You might find out that you're addicted to a certain behaviour and have to take it to a deeper level to resolve it. Or you might discover that your goals completely change as you change. What you thought you wanted might not be what you want after all . . . or what you wanted to achieve at the start of the journey could transform as you progress.

For example, if you want a fantastic body, you're going to have to give up sitting in front of the television night after night and do some hard work in the gym! You might discover on your journey that relaxing with your family is more important to you than hardcore exercise, or that your plans for reaching the top in your career may be superseded by your desire to spend more time with your family . . . or the other way around. Awakening is like rebuilding the puzzle of your life: you have to dismantle the current jigsaw so that you have space for new pieces.

Albert Einstein said the definition of insanity is 'doing the same thing over and over again and expecting different results.' If you want a different outcome, you have to take different actions. And that means change!

CHAPTER THREE

Preparing For The Journey Into The Land Of The Awakened

'The only true wisdom is in knowing you know nothing.'

Socrates

The many spokes in the Wheel of Life allow it to turn smoothly: relationships, health, emotions, finances, religion, career and purpose to name just a few. In the same way that your physical, mental, emotional and spiritual energies are intertwined and interdependent, the same is true of the Wheel of Life: when one area isn't working properly, it impacts the others. So when you begin to experience your Awakening you'll find that working on one zone may have a knock-on effect on all the others. You may work to clear a particular issue from your life, but to move on from it will likely mean working on something else, probably unexpectedly.

For example, if you find public speaking difficult then it may be holding back your career. Working on that single aspect will also transform the energy of your self-esteem and confidence, and so attract new people and opportunities into your life. When you work on your relationship with one aspect of yourself and it clears, then you make space for a new one to show up.

I believe that all of life is relationship. If your health isn't working then your relationship with health is not working, if your finances are a mess then your relationship with money is a mess. Even when your relationships themselves are not giving you happiness, it's your relationship with relationships that requires attention. So before beginning your Awakening journey, you need to find out what your Wheel of Life currently looks like by using the following exercise. In this way, you'll start to get a tangible idea of what it is that you want to improve, so that at the end of your journey you'll be able to look back and see what is possible as a result of applying the Nine Principles of Awakening. For this reason, I also suggest starting an Awakening journal where you can record your experiences.

Wheel of Life

Answer the following questions and make a note of your answers and scores for each one:

- How do you currently rate your relationship with your partner? Give it a score between 0–10, with 0 if you don't have one and 10 if your relationship is exactly where you want it to be. If your relationship isn't working, why do you think that is?
- How do you currently rate your health? Give it a score between 0–10, with 0 for intensely ill and 10 if you're completely happy with it. If you're not satisfied with your health, what needs to change?
- How do you rate your current finances? Give them a score between 0–10, with 0 if you're in real difficulties and 10 if you're completely satisfied. If you have a low score, why do you think this is?
- Finally, take some time to write down any other spokes in the Wheel of Life that you would like to work on.

Now that you have identified where you are, and have given possible reasons for why things are this way, it's time to set your intention for your Awakening. Make sure to take a note of your answers.

- What is it that you specifically want to create as a result of going through your Awakening?

Preparing for the journey ahead

The journey you are undertaking may prove to be one of the most important in your life. This is about going inward and waking up to the truth of who you are. Like any other journey, preparation is crucial. After taking thousands of people through my workshops and transformational weekends, I've come to realize that preparation is the first step toward success. In order to make the most of your journey, I invite you to take the following suggestions on board:

Be open-minded
There is nothing more dangerous than a closed mind. The three words that keep it closed are, 'I know that . . .' The information in this book is not new because the knowledge has been around for thousands of years, so think of it as your chance to re-experience, re-visit, re-discover, re-instate and re-validate what you know to be true. Stay open and receptive and you'll be able to learn and use what you know to move up to the next level.

Fully participate
Create a sacred space in your life by giving yourself some time each day or week to work with each of the principles of Awakening. In this way, you'll be able to participate fully in the process and get the most out of all the exercises and tools and the journey as a whole.

Appreciate

In order to speed up your Awakening, learn to appreciate both the good aspects and the bad aspects of your life because, as you will find out, our challenges, mistakes and difficulties are the catalysts that drive us toward changing for the better.

Awakening journal

As mentioned above (see page 21), start a journal where you can record your insights and so you can look back and see how far you have come. The day-to-day progress of your journey will inspire you to continue until being Awake becomes your natural state.

Compassion

Throughout your journey show compassion to yourself and others, and trust that whatever is coming up is a benevolent guide taking you safely into unexplored territory.

Take responsibility

The word responsibility means your ability to respond rather than blame, so when you take responsibility you take charge of your own reactions, regardless of anyone else's action. No one is the keeper of your emotions; we create our own experiences and perceptions of the world. You will be creating your own experience through this book.

Entering the Land of Awakening

The journey of Awakening is similar to moving to a new country: it has its own laws, language, principles and even beliefs. For this reason, each of the Nine Principles is a combination of the process of Awakening, stories, case studies and exercises. To help you get the maximum out of your journey through each principle here follows some of the things to look out for:

Questions as catalysts

Use the questions throughout the book as catalysts to delve into your true self; they are designed to help you shed your old programming (beliefs and values), so record your answers in your Awakening journal.

Daily Practices

Most of the exercises are very simple and short but you will instantly feel the profound results they bring on a physical, mental, emotional and spiritual level. These Daily Practices will support you as you imbue your life with energy that is more aligned to your true desires and help you to breathe in new life.

Divine Magic Statements

Any statement or truth that your mind accepts as being truth quickly becomes part of its programming or energy. Use the Divine Magic Statements as you would a mantra, affirmation, meditation or prayer: reflect upon them and repeat them often – particularly when you're facing challenges or are unsure how to proceed. I've infused each of them with love to help you feel energized and supported throughout the day.

Cloaks for your journey

The main qualities you will need on your journey are:

- The intention to change your life.
- Permission to access all parts of you.
- Faith to know that you are loved.
- Courage to feel the fear and still keep going.
- Perseverance to stay on the path when the journey gets tough.

Connecting to Source

I come from a Muslim family and was taught to believe in Allah (the Source), a Day of Judgment, Heaven and Hell. But the more I explored the spiritual realm, the more I understood that the Source is the same for everyone, but different people give it different names – God, Allah, Buddha, Krishna, the light, the Universe, consciousness – they all seem to be describing the same thing.

The beauty of Awakening is that it doesn't rely on you believing in the Source or any spiritual being, deity or all-powerful God. It is more about being open and receptive to discovering and accessing any information that puts you in the right space and leads you to healing. Now I see religion or spiritual practice more as a mode of transportation to takes us to the Source. Just as we can choose how we're going to reach a particular destination – plane, ferry, bus, bicycle or even on foot – the same goes for religious or spiritual beliefs; they help us reach our destination, which is to meet ourselves as an expression of the Divine.

Dressing for your journey

The following meditation will support you on your journey, and I encourage you to use it as often as you can.

Find a space where you can be undisturbed and peaceful. Take a few deep in-breaths and focus on your breathing to help quiet your mind and become present.

Then, when you are ready, imagine a wonderful wave of relaxation starting at the top of your head and moving through your body until it undulates all the way down to the tips of your toes. Let every nerve and cell in your body be bathed in this beautiful wave of calmness.

As you relax more deeply, imagine you are in front of a mysterious wooden cupboard with a gold handle

– this is where your Awakening cloaks live. As you open the cupboard you see ornate and colourful cloaks on hangers. Some have names written on them: intention, permission, courage, faith and perseverance; and there are others there too, including determination, compassion, truth and flow. A few have no names and these are omni-cloaks that can embody whatever quality you require most for your journey.

Go inside the cupboard and choose whichever cloak you need most. The beauty of these cloaks is that they are invisible and once you are wearing one it will instantly nourish you with the quality you choose.

Once you have chosen your cloak, put it on and imagine how having that quality will help you through the coming days and weeks. Walk around and experience how it feels to wear this cloak. Visualize being in a situation that you usually find challenging and difficult, and how wearing this cloak will help you to respond in the best way.

When you are ready, end the meditation and enjoy the rest of your day imbued with the energy of your cloak.

The Nine Principles

The Nine Principles form a bridge between where you are right now and where you want to be. The journey in between is one of truth. Truth is a source of transformation, which is why people often fear it. Truth causes change. It is not possible to absorb the power of truth and have your life remain the same. In some way, at some level, every truth changes your life. Truth has the power to heal and cleanse your soul. That is why you have to build up the stamina to manage truth, as your life will never be the same again once you start the Awakening process.

When you are ready, turn the page . . .

PART II

Awakening:
The Nine Principles

'The principles are a bridge to an Awakened life.
Working with them will bring you closer to a life of
ease, grace and magic!'

Sidra Jafri

Ask Quality Questions

'The unexamined life is not worth living.'
Socrates

As we grow into adulthood and beyond, we often find that life speeds up with each year. We get more responsibilities and more to do as each day passes and accordingly we accept more and question less. Life becomes what it is – even if it means we are not being our true self or living our life's purpose. When we activate the first principle, Ask Quality Questions, it causes us to observe our life – our beliefs, behaviours, emotions and so on. Questions force us to pause, go inside and intuit the answer. What you find there may surprise or even shock you, but you will have started to see the truth and from that place you can only grow.

Creation of beliefs, values and behaviours

When we were newborns we believed we were the entire world. We didn't yet understand that our arms and legs belonged to us or that those people over there were separate from us. We were part of the fabric of the Universe, the Source, and it was part of us. Later we learned what our mouth, hands, feet and eyes were for, and the colours, shapes and sounds around us morphed into the separate forms of our family and our home. We became separated from the Source, too, as it became something that resided out there in society not in our hearts.

As we grew into toddlers we also discovered that we had less control over the world than we thought and were entirely dependent on others for our survival. When we were ready to speak, we experienced an overwhelming urge to assert ourselves as an independent being. To survive on our own, we had to explore the environment and we questioned everything to find out exactly what kind of a world we were in.

Enquiring into the status quo of our world is crucial for our survival. The more we understand about our environment, the more informed our decisions and judgments will be. But the search for knowledge goes beyond taking care of our needs for food, clothing, comfort and shelter. We find explanations deeply comforting as they give us a sense of control and understanding of the world. There's a pleasure in discovering new ideas or information and sharing knowledge with other people. We ask questions of others because if we don't know something, they might.

Human beings have a limited perception of reality, but giving meaning to what happens to us helps fill in the gaps in our knowledge and broadens our perspective. Naming things, reasoning and giving things a purpose all help us navigate the chaos of reality. To make sense of our world we must ask questions of it.

We also live in a rewards-based society where we are given incentives to search for and give the correct answers. From our school days through to finding our careers and beyond, we are applauded for our ability to create wise or intelligent solutions. When we don't manage to come up with a satisfactory answer, or are unable to convince anyone we have one, we are likely to feel foolish and, conversely, when we ask too many questions we're often told to 'be quiet' or 'don't ask why' – sometimes that's because the people we were asking didn't know the answers either!

So instead of asking 'why' we started to follow what we were told to do without questioning 'why?' As adults we are expected to be more experienced and knowledgeable about life but often we would rather be left in the dark and pretend we know something than risk being laughed at or rejected for not being wise. Worrying that our ignorance will be discovered may lead us to fear asking questions altogether. But going through the motions of life, accepting others' beliefs and practices as your own without questioning 'why' means you're not experiencing life as fully as you could be.

I believe that everything our ancestors did in their time was right for them in their current time but, as time moves on humanity evolves, so it's our job to update our actions, beliefs and practices, and align them with our current timeline. We need to ask 'why' we are doing certain actions, as the following story demonstrates.

THE LOBSTER'S TAIL

One day a child was watching her mother prepare a lobster for lunch. 'Why are you cutting off its tail?' she asked. 'Hmm,' replied her mother, as she dropped the pieces into boiling water, 'Now you ask, I'm not sure why. It's something your Grandma showed me how to do.' Curious, the little girl ran off to find her grandmother. 'Grandma! Why do you cut off the lobster's tail before you boil it?' Her grandmother said, 'No idea, to be honest. My mother always did it like that.' The girl found her great-grandmother in her rocking chair. The old lady laughed. 'Do they still do that? I just cut it up to fit it into my pan.'

Ask and you shall receive

Our mind is a meaning-creating device, designed to ask questions and to answer them. It is likely that you have experienced the power of questions many times, especially when someone has asked you a question, which you previously knew the answer to, but have forgotten. It's likely that you shrugged your shoulders in response so that you could get on with your day, but that question hooks your mind, even if you thought you'd disregarded it. A few days later, the answer might pop into your head when you least expected it. Unanswered questions get filed in your subconscious, the submerged part of your mental iceberg, and this is where between 80 and 90 percent of your mental processes occur, quietly unknown to you on a conscious level.

Our conscious mind deals with the here and now but it is not equipped to process the vast amount of information we constantly encounter. In his book, *Flow: The Psychology of Happiness*, the distinguished Hungarian psychology professor Mihaly Csikszentmihalyi suggests that our mind receives at least two million bits of information per second. This bombardment is overwhelming for the conscious part of the mind, so it creates a system to filter the information to avoid overload. It deletes, distorts and generalizes the information, and out of two million only 134 bits actually go in. Which 134 bits go in is dependent on the programs (beliefs) that are installed by our family, language, religion, teachers, friends and environment.

Unanswered questions sit in the subterranean depths of our subconscious as we scan for a reason, memory or meaning that satisfies our query in the most appropriate way. When our brain finds the solution, it pops back into our awareness, often when our conscious mind isn't terribly busy. That's why we often remember things when we're doing something that takes little conscious attention or in a meditative or flow state, such as driving the same route home from work or daydreaming while getting the ironing done.

The feeling you have when something is at the tip of your tongue or that you know something but can't place it yet, is because you know on a subconscious level that you have the answer somewhere, it's just that it's on a shelf you can't reach for now.

Why, why, why?

When we ask a question such as, 'Why did I fail?' the Internet search engine of our mind will look for all the likely causes and reasons associated with the circumstances in question. Our thoughts might produce answers such as, 'You were too lazy,' or 'You're a bad communicator,' and so on. Just like Google, the answers we find are limited to what we ask. For example, if you type 'Chicago' into Google you'll receive thousands of pages relating to that word, but if you want to know whether you need to pack un umbrella on your next trip, typing in 'Chicago weather forecast' is going to give you much more useful results.

In the same way, making your question more relevant will yield answers that can get you out of a rut. Rephrasing, 'Why did I fail?' to 'What have I learned from this experience?' will give you answers such as, 'Leaving things to the last minute is not healthy,' or 'I must trust my inner feelings more.' This is information you can learn from and will move you forward.

The quality of your question mirrors the answer you receive.

Reasons versus results

To make your questions work harder, you need to think about how they are constructed: what are you really asking? The majority of questions consist of two types:

- Reason-led questions: Why? Where?
- Results-led questions: How? What?

Both types of question are important and serve great purpose when used in the right context. Reason-led questions give us an explanation for why and where a situation is happening in our lives? Results-led questions make us aware how or what to do to resolve an issue or offer an answer that moves us into a positive direction.

A question opens the doors of possibility to explore. When we look beneath the truth of what's holding us back, we might discover underlying past memories and events where we had made a certain decision that has created the current issue in our lives. But if you have only been asking yourself 'why' questions, you'll be getting reasons but not solutions.

For example, when I was working on reaching my ideal weight. I recognized that one of the major challenges I faced was eating a healthy diet. Asking 'Why do I end up eating unhealthily?' gave me the answer, 'It's easier and more comfortable.' Then I changed my question and asked, 'How can I eat more healthily?' The answer came into my head in the form of a thought, 'Buy more fruits and vegetables instead of cookies and cakes.'

Asking quality questions prods your automatic unconscious responses back into life.

You might find you're sticking rigidly to a belief that helped you survive in the past, and need to ask results-led questions that move you away from your usual responses. Shift the question and think about how you can change a 'why' or 'where' question into a 'how' or 'what' question. Instead of saying, 'Why do I have no money?' ask, 'How can I earn more money?' Or replace, 'Why am I not attracting a new partner?' with 'How can I invite a new partner into my life?'

Asking quality questions has helped me to manifest the most amazing clients, friends and business opportunities into my life. After walking out on my marriage, I was struggling financially and couldn't pay my bills. I would ask, 'What space do I need to be in to allow a paying client to show up?' As a result I would often receive emails from friends saying that they had just referred someone to me. I learned that asking results-led questions keeps us open to the possibility of something new and different appearing.

Asking the Source, 'Show me the way' or 'What is the best possible way?' has always proved enlightening for me. Whenever I feel down I ask, 'How does it get any better than this?' – meaning show me any feeling that is better than feeling like this. Simply by continuing to ask that question, we can slowly and gradually start shifting our focus and feeling better. Now when I feel really happy I ask, 'How does it get even better than this?'

Mastering language

To master the question is to honour the power of words that we use in our daily language. Words are magical tools of divinity, and each word has a unique energetic imprint. Words bring our thoughts and feelings to life; they give our ideas substance and a personality. These spoken and written symbols of human language enable us to describe all things, so we can communicate ideas, feelings and meanings to each other. All our conscious thoughts consist of words as part of language: descriptions, symbols and intentions that we choose to define our feelings and the world around us. Therefore it is completely within our power to change the words and change the meanings we give to any situation we find ourselves in.

Choosing uplifting, thought-provoking or optimistic words to describe a difficult emotion or challenging situation changes our perception of it, and therefore our reaction to it. For example, if you tell yourself that you got out of the wrong side of the bed this morning and that nothing is going to go well today, then you'll spend the day looking for things that confirm that perception. Just as if you tell yourself it's going to be a particularly lucky day, then you'll see the smallest thing as a positive omen. It is the intention behind the words that counts.

Our choice of words also affects other people's lives by creating powerful emotional reactions: inspiring or galvanizing people into action for good or evil. If you are in the habit (or have learned from others) to label uncomfortable feelings such as fear, anger and jealousy with negative or unhelpful words such as 'pain' or 'bad' then those emotions don't have the chance to become anything different. If you grew up in a family that had problems dealing with anger, you may have learned to label anger as something that needs to be 'kept hidden' or as 'destructive', when in fact anger can be an extremely motivating, cathartic and insightful emotion once we learn to express it in a way that serves us.

Words give us the power to diagnose what we need in order to make sound decisions and asking quality questions will tell us if we are going in the right direction. Just by changing the words you use to construct your thoughts completely transforms your intention and therefore the results; and this little profound truth can change your entire being.

A BLIND MAN'S STORY

Recently I came across a YouTube video by Andrea Gardner, author of *Change Your Words, Change Your World*, which demonstrates the power of language and our ability to change its energy. You might want to go and find the video and take a look at it. It's about a blind man begging on the side of the road with a sign that reads, 'I'm blind. Please help!' He sits there for hours and most people pay him scant attention. Then a woman comes by and changes the writing on his sign. As soon as she leaves, people started pouring coins into his bowl. Later that evening the woman returns, and the blind man asks her what she did to his sign. She responds, 'I wrote the same – just different words.' The sign now read, 'It's a beautiful day and I can't see it!'

Creating healing statements

Choose the statements that you make about yourself carefully. You might be inadvertently stating things about yourself that are having a negative effect. For example, if you don't like to appear materialistic because you feel unfairly judged by others, you might find yourself frequently saying something like, 'Oh, I don't care about money.' What you mean is you don't like to appear greedy. Money probably makes your life much easier! But if you keep telling yourself that you don't care about it, don't expect it to do you any favours. What you hear yourself saying can become what you believe.

Words heal, words harm, and they have the potential to change the path of your life. You can use words to create heaven on earth or you can use words to turn your life into a living hell. I believe one of the most powerful starting phrases is 'I am . . .' Whatever you say after 'I am' defines you and your state of being: 'I am grateful', 'I am angry', 'I am always late', 'I am gorgeous', 'I am clumsy' and so on.

Use words that uplift you and raise your energy. In stressful times you can use your statements to give you courage, strength or comfort: 'I am brave', 'I am loved', 'I am creative', 'I am inspiring', 'I am responsible', 'I am peaceful', 'I am focused'. Choose qualities that are true of you, as an individual, and that you would like to demonstrate in your life.

What is your language saying?

Many people use language about themselves that does not serve them. When you dig deeper into your 'I am' statements by asking quality questions such as, 'Who does this opinion belong to?' or 'Where is this coming from?', you can trace the original point of creation to another commonly used phrase: 'You are . . .'

Our parents, teachers, peers and authority figures often used this phrase to start a description of us. When the description that follows is life-affirming and positive, it creates positive healthy energy within us and we take that with us into adulthood. But too often the most influential people in our lives, our families and teachers, give us less helpful descriptions, such as, 'You are silly', 'You are shy', 'You are fat', 'You are dumb' or 'You are lazy', which are converted by us into, 'I am silly', 'I am shy', 'I am fat', 'I am dumb' or 'I am lazy'. This is because, as I described earlier (see page 17), as children we accept the words of authority figures, such as our parents, as being all-powerful and don't question their truth. This leads to us to believe that all these messages are sacred and we live them as though they are true.

What we believe to be true creates our reality and gives us a story to inhabit.

Daily Practice: Make a new statement

Find a pen and your Awakening journal and write, 'I am . . .' at the top of the sheet. Now scribble down at least 20 words that spring to mind, but don't analyze them too closely.

The key here is to write without thinking about it, to channel what's at the bottom of your psyche, rather than what's on the tip of your tongue.

Now look at your results.

- Which words did you choose to describe yourself?
- Are you surprised by anything you wrote?
- Why?
- Is there anything there that you wish to change?
- Which words will you use to describe yourself instead?

Write down your new statements about yourself and repeat them whenever you need to reinforce your new message.

Question your story

We all love hearing and telling stories, and the ones we tell others about ourselves are especially revealing. When you recount a tale of something that has happened to you, your inquisitive imagination is irresistibly drawn to fill in the gaps to give it more interest, make it funny, dramatic or more compelling. The story of how you battled an illness, told your boss to get lost or dealt with an exceptionally challenging person will of course be based on truth, but we like to mould the facts to suit our own agenda, to give the story more power or to confirm or deny something we want to highlight in our personality. The act of giving your story purpose, reason and structure makes it appear so real that you begin to believe in it too; it becomes part of you.

If what you are saying about yourself is negative, you can become trapped inside your own thought creation.

I believe we all have the power to change our ideas of ourselves by questioning the validity of our behaviour to break free from our self-imposed beliefs, as Jayne's story demonstrates.

LEARNING TO TRUST AGAIN

Jayne was in her mid-thirties and very quiet. She described how she had always found it 'very difficult' to trust and relate to others. She went from a tiny school to another school of 3,000 pupils with massive walls, long corridors and large classrooms. To her, it felt like a prison and the other kids bullied her mercilessly. She was naive and couldn't understand why the other kids weren't nice to her. Jayne described how she was shocked by their mistreatment of her and retreated inside. She was unprepared for this mean new world and felt abandoned by her friends and family.

She spent the next four school years in a permanent state of anxiety and became reclusive. Bullied for her shyness, Jayne described how it had made her mistrustful of new people and she struggled to form any close relationships. 'Strangers are trouble' became her motto. As she grew into adulthood, she prided herself on her independence and not needing anyone else but deep down she felt isolated. Then she met a man but when he tried to get too close to her she put up a wall to protect herself: 'I could tell he wanted to be my friend, we had loads in common and up until I'd thought he was getting too close, we'd had a real laugh together.' Changing seemed to be 'too big a thing', and she didn't really know where to start.

Using the Awakening process she started to question by asking, 'What am I hiding from?' It made her question her behaviour and she started to see how self-defeating it was becoming. Jayne realized that she had allowed her bad experiences at school to colour the rest of her life with its negativity. After Awakening, she described how her outlook had changed, 'Now I'm looking at life through a brand new lens, one that's not clouded by my own judgments.'

Our story exists so that we can make sense of what has happened to us. Jayne carried the trauma of her bullying around for 20 years. The event itself and all the people involved were long gone from her life but she clung on to the story because it gave her the identity of 'being independent' and 'not needing anyone else', without that story she didn't know who she would become. But we are not the sum of just what has happened to us. By questioning the validity of our story and its relevance in the present, we can let go of past hurt, disappointment, anger and pain, and welcome new experiences into our lives.

Most of the time we don't even know who we are without our family, friends, work, religion and usual environment. We identify ourselves with what we do for a living, which religion or culture we belong to or who our family and friends are. I hear many people say, 'I am a doctor', 'I am an accountant', 'I am a teacher', but the truth is that we are not what we do; these are just different roles we play. We are more than just that and asking questions expand our identities so that we become more than who we think we are.

It requires courage, faith and tenacity to question your identity. If you are not happy in any area of your life, asking quality questions will help you break free from the false identities you have created from all those 'I am . . .' and 'You are . . .' phrases and get back to the real you – the one that knows how to be a joyful being.

> Ask yourself, 'What is it in me that is causing this situation?'

Your default questions

Deep down inside, beneath our conscious awareness, questions constantly run in the background of our mind. I call these our 'default questions' and they form the basis of our emotions. Knowing your default questions can give you real insight into why you might be in a particular situation or why it's proving difficult to move forward. You may discover that you have been asking yourself the same things for years and the same answer has been keeping you stuck.

Discovering your default questions and then rewording them from reason-led questions ('why' or 'where') to results-led queries ('how' or 'what') takes your mind in a new direction and allows your subconscious to create a different solution – one that isn't hardwired to go for your usual subconsciously stored response.

Daily Practice: Default questions

To discover your default questions, use the following process with each of your default questions and afterwards record your answers in your Awakening journal.

Close your eyes and take a few deep breaths in and out, and bring your mind into the present by simply focusing on your breathing. When you are ready ask:

- What questions do I ask the most?

Give yourself some time and let the answers bubble up from your subconscious as naturally as possible. Don't try to analyze them; just let them float up to your conscious mind. Did just one answer come to you? Perhaps you had a few questions that you regularly ask. Write down the answers.

Now it's time to transform that question into one that serves you better by making a conscious decision to change your default question. Choose questions that will lead you to take charge and inspire you to take action. For example, you might ask:

- How can I make this work?
- What am I learning as a result of this experience?
- What would it take for me to achieve the results that I want?

Make sure to take a note of your questions. When you hear a default question arise in your mind, replace it with your new, more creative question.

At first you'll need to make a conscious decision to ask a more creative question but after a few repetitions it will become your new default question and will serve you better in resolving the issue.

Do this exercise for each of your default questions as you recognize them.

Whose energy are you in?

I described earlier (see page 8) that everything is energy and that we can see, feel and perceive energy everywhere, including from other human beings. Energy flows and exchanges between people, which means that we regularly absorb each other's emotions, thoughts and opinions. This means that sometimes the way we behave has less to do with our own feelings and more with how people around us are thinking and feeling. Believe it or not, most of the way we act is a result of us living according to what other people believe us to be like.

In a famous study looking at the how the intentions behind words can influence matter, Dr Masaru Emoto, author of *Messages from Water and the Universe*, conducted several studies of how different words, images and messages affected molecular structures. Using bottles of distilled water, he recorded how each responded to different emotive pictures, sounds, words and phrases, such as 'thank you' or 'you disgust me' to try to influence the water's behaviour before freezing it. Afterwards he photographed the water crystals and noted that the water that had received positive intentions created beautiful geometric crystals while those that had received negative intentions were marked by distorted, random patterns. Dr Emoto maintains that the intention behind the words on the labels changed the water's structure, effectively proving how it's possible for intentions to transform matter.

I believe that our physical body is the key to unlimited knowledge about us and at a cellular level it remembers every event that has ever happened. It holds the key to all of our locked doors to health, wealth and optimum happiness. This has particular significance when we think that 80 percent of our body is made up of water (our brains even more). Dr Emoto's findings suggest that our thoughts and intentions can have a direct effect on our body and mind because if water holds memories, then our body contains the record of all the events that we have experienced. No event ever goes unrecorded.

For example, if your parents have always told you that you are the entertainer of the family then it's likely that you'll try to make people smile, even if you long for someone to empathize with your problems. You might be chirpy and talkative at work but if your partner thinks 'you are boring' then you may start to feel down and quiet when you are with them. This is because you have entered the 'zone' of their beliefs about you and you are just slipping back into the role you have been assigned.

It is also possible, because we are all energetic beings, to pick up from someone else's emotions. You may have experienced a time when someone else's bad temper or heightened emotions have 'rubbed off' on you and left you feeling irritated and upset even though their emotions may not have been directed at you personally; or someone else's road rage leaves you feeling rattled and angry when you're usually a calm driver. This is the power of being in someone else's energy.

Daily Practice: Whose feeling is this?

Once you start to recognize that you are acting out others' feelings or beliefs, you can change its energy by using quality questions to recognize where the belief is coming from. When you feel an emotion that you want to address ask:

- 'Who does this feeling belong to?'

Asking this question will give you a clue as to whether what you are feeling belongs to you or has been triggered by someone else or you have picked up on someone else's emotions. Once we access this information we can imbue our cells, our minds and our language with more positive helpful energy that is more aligned with our true self.

Questions stretch minds

When something in our life is not working, it's usually our belief around that situation that requires attention. A quality question stretches the mind and examines the basis of that belief, which is usually a result of the meaning we have given to an event. For example, if your partner says, 'You don't love me anymore', you might reply, 'How do you know?' This type of question will lead them to think about the meaning they have attributed to your actions that made them think in that particular way. If they respond by saying, 'Because you don't call me', you can offer up another question such as, 'What if me not calling you means I trust you and want to give you space?' Altering your question affects the action you might take, and therefore the quality of the results. Giving yourself a more positive vision of the future by making these simple changes can turn your life around.

Ask yourself, 'Whom does this belief belong to?' Your answers will help you separate your own beliefs from those that you have inherited from others.

Daily Practice: Powerful questions to challenge issues

Asking quality questions has brought the right people and situations into my life exactly when I've needed them. I have distilled the knowledge I've discovered into a few powerful questions that will allow abundance to flow into your life.

Pick an issue in your life that you are finding challenging. Then write down any thoughts and feelings connected with it in your Awakening journal. Be as open-minded as possible about what comes up. Now ask a question from the list below that best fits your situation.

- What contribution can I make to enjoy a fun and phenomenal day?
- Who can contribute toward my business project?
- What space do I need to be in to allow a perfect relationship to show up in my reality?
- What space can I create to allow more money, more joy and more love to show up in my life?
- What contribution can I make to the consciousness of the planet?

Your question should be followed by what I call a 'clearing statement' because the answers can bring up fears, judgments, beliefs and past experiences that are stopping you from transforming the energy you need in your life. By using the following clearing statement you will make space for new opportunities to be created with ease and grace.

'Everything that stops [*insert the issue*] from happening, I release you from my energy. From all levels, dimensions and timeframes right to the point of creation. Please remove and clear all traumatic memories relating to past rejection, abandonment and fear of being in love. From the cells, the DNA structure at all levels, dimensions and timeframes. Thank you.'

Ask your questions wisely. Like mastering any new skill, it takes time, practice, perseverance and most importantly patience. The more you practise the more profound your results will be. Get into the habit of using your questioning skills by using them in everyday situations. Stop shrugging your shoulders when your boss gives you a difficult task or accepting excuses from people to avoid a confrontation. Asking a well-timed question can sometimes surprise people into giving an honest answer because they don't have time to think of an alternative.

THE CUNNING STOREKEEPER

A certain man had many problems in his life and couldn't seem to move past them. One day he happened to pass a shop and noticed a sign in the window: 'Special Offer: Any Two Questions Answered. Just 10 Gold Coins!' The man immediately went in and handed over the money. 'I hope you can help me,' he said. 'But all the same isn't 10 gold coins rather expensive for just two questions?'

The shopkeeper replied, 'Correct! Now ask me your second question.'

ACTIVATING THE FIRST PRINCIPLE: ASK QUALITY QUESTIONS

The first step of the Awakening journey, Ask Quality Questions, takes a great deal of courage and perseverance. Questioning the source of your beliefs, values, behaviours and self-perceptions, you suddenly awake to the fact that you didn't create your world and your life is not your own. The right question at the right time then serves as a wake-up call to your subconscious mind and you can then choose to look for new answers to old issues. Questioning your beliefs, behaviours and emotions, and how you use language to tell stories to and about yourself, you start to see others and yourself afresh.

In the next principle, Work On You, we'll explore how taking care of yourself can transform all your relationships and allow your truth to shine.

Divine Magic Statement

I ask quality questions and receive answers with ease and grace.

Work On You

'The best way to make someone happy is to be happy. You can't give what you don't have.'

Sidra Jafri

For most people the phrase 'self-sacrifice' conjures up an image of charity, caring and selflessness, and don't misunderstand me, those are all amazing qualities. However, the true meaning of self-sacrifice is looking after everyone else without paying attention to our own needs, and this isn't good for our emotional wellbeing. It results in resentment, disappointment and even physical symptoms such as feeling fatigued and lacklustre. The second principle, Work On You, puts you at the top of the agenda because when you work on yourself, you work on everybody else too. When you learn to accept, forgive and love yourself for who you are, only then will you be able to love and accept others for who they are, which will result in more loving and harmonious relationships.

The real meaning of selfish

'You are being so selfish! At least think about your boys! You are bringing shame to the family.' These were the words I kept hearing over and over again when I decided to end my marriage. The constant pressure from my family to reconsider my decision made me feel guilty, as though I were doing something wrong. I felt devastated by all the accusations levelled at me as a result of wanting to live my own truth. The only thing that kept me going through this, the toughest phase of my life, was a verse from my favourite poem:

> *'I want to know if you can disappoint another to be true to yourself. If you can bear the accusation of betrayal and not betray your own soul . . .'*
> *The Invitation,* Oriah the Mountain Dreamer

In my experience, many people have a warped view of what being selfish actually means. Most of us assume that selfish means placing your needs first, at the expense of others. But there are many times in life when you must put yourself first. I knew that if I had stayed in my marriage I would have died. But getting divorced meant I had to think about myself: my wellbeing before everyone else's. I wouldn't have been able to continue otherwise. The decision I made was between my kids having a 'dead married mother' or an 'alive divorced mother.' It was a no-brainer.

One of the most fascinating things I learned during my divorce was how people's opinions of what I was doing varied. Some people thought I was being terribly selfish, while others turned me into a role model and used me as their inspiration to break free from what was keeping them stuck in their lives too.

Forgiving and loving yourself to love and forgive others

Putting others' needs before your own is usually a result of witnessing your parents' 'people-pleasing' program. This is a very common program and is found across all cultures to varying degrees. In collective societies, it plays a bigger role where the culture of looking after elderly family members is prevalent. Children watch their parents disregard their own needs to put grandparents first and grow up thinking that's how life is lived; they disregard their own desires and needs as unimportant compared to the people around them.

Just as a naked man can't give you his shirt, you can't love anyone else if you don't love yourself.

Denying our own needs creates conflicts as they cannot be ignored and often come back in disguise – sometimes, in the form of physical illness, which in my opinion is a subconscious way of looking for love. If we are focused on looking after other people all the time, we don't have time to look after ourselves. Working on ourselves gives us permission to turn that caring, sensitivity back toward our own heart. It doesn't mean we are more important than anyone else – just as important as them.

The world won't crumble

Helping the people we love is one of the most rewarding things to do in life. When you know you are appreciated and you love the person you are assisting, there is a beautiful, nourishing and healing energy exchange that occurs. What a wonderful feeling to know you have made someone you care about feel better by being there when they needed you.

When you aren't appreciated and feel like you are being taken for granted or are being bullied into spending your time helping other people then feelings of resentment can build up, which can make you feel heavy and drained, and creates a negative energy exchange between you and the other person. It is in these circumstances that the second principle, Work On You, really makes a difference. When you stop taking on responsibility for others' worries and needs you will find that something wonderful happens – the world does not crumble! If needing more time for yourself means you can't babysit your niece or travel across town to feed your friend's cat or volunteer at a local charity cake sale, the planet will still turn.

The Universe doesn't need you for it to survive. But it would rather you were happy because every feeling you have, every thought and action, has an impact on everything else. If you feel good then you make a conscious decision to send out your positive energy and thoughts to those who need them, as the man in the following story knew how to do.

TWO NEIGHBOURS

There was once a man who seemed to have everything: a well-paid job, a caring wife and kind, studious and grateful children. His neighbour, on the other hand, was the exact opposite: he had no job, he couldn't get on with his wife and his children were always causing trouble. The rich man was known in the town for being very devout. 'He must really understand how to talk to God,' said the townsfolk. 'He spends so long in the temple and look what he has received in return!'

One day a group of townsfolk sneaked up on the rich man in the temple, to try to hear exactly what he was asking God for, so that they might benefit in the same way. To their surprise all they could hear was the man requesting God to help his poor neighbour. Afterwards, they questioned him in the street. 'Why were you asking for that wastrel to become wealthy? And for his wife to love him? And for those annoying kids to be happy? What are you, some kind of saint?'

The man laughed. 'No, I'm no saint! Do you really think I was praying for him? Look, my life should be very enjoyable. Thank God, my kids are doing well, my wife is happy with our life and I've managed to put some money away. The only fly in the ointment is that neighbour of mine! He's fighting with his wife day and night, and when they're not fighting the kids are squabbling. Those children don't do anything useful, they just damage my property and make noise. So I ask God to give my neighbour some money, so that he can send his children to school. I ask God to send love to the marriage so that the two of them will stop arguing and I can finally get some sleep at night. And most of all I ask God to send my neighbour a job, so that he will get out the house and stop bothering me with his endless complaints. So you see that I haven't been praying for my neighbour at all – only for myself!'

Making me happy is good!

The truth is that everyone in this world is responsible for creating their own experience of life and once you recognize that, you can take charge of your own happiness without feeling guilty that it is somehow wrong to think about your own wellbeing. If you spend your energy trying to live up to others' expectations or by hoping to impress someone who never notices, it's going to be a long fight. Taking on other peoples' causes, or solving their problems, is another way of making sure that your needs are met last, if at all.

Everyone is looking for ways to be happy, whether they realize it or not. Even behaviour that appears to be counterproductive has a perceived advantage. For example, the parents who scold their kids for misbehaving or push them too hard to study often want to be appreciated for being a 'good' parent. At work, going out of your way for a colleague at your own expense might be a way of gaining their acknowledgment, but if you don't appreciate what you're doing on a conscious level, you might end up resenting that colleague for their 'unwarranted' requests.

Everything you do, you do to make yourself happier. Once you acknowledge this important truth about life then the burden of being responsible for everyone else's happiness will lift and you'll stop being needy for praise and attention from everyone else.

Daily Practice: Being the CEO of you

Sometimes people are subscribed to their friends' problems and vice versa; they exchange personal challenges and later feel drained as a result. It is now time to step into the shoes of the CEO of you and cancel your subscription to other people's issues because you're not helping them or yourself.

Close your eyes and take a few deep breaths in and out, and bring your mind into the present by simply focusing on your breathing. When you are ready, start by using the 'dressing for your journey' meditation on page 48, and put on the cloak of compassion.

Now, think of the people who drain you with their problems and needs, imagine them seated in front of you in a large room with a spotlight on each person.

Say to them silently but with compassion: 'Please cancel my subscription to your issues. Forgive me for wanting to move on from you and I forgive you for using me as a sounding board for your problems. We are all free now. May you find what you are looking for. Thank you.'

When you finish saying these words, just imagine the people seated in front of you standing up and leaving the room one by one. As a result of this process, in your external reality, you will start to notice that those people will gradually stop unloading their woes onto your shoulders. And when they do, they'll sense that your energy is different, and may look for someone else on whom to unload their burdens.

Being the CEO of you also means that you need to release all the people you have been offloading your own issues onto.

So think of all those people you have used as an emotional dumping yard. Imagine you're back in the room with the spotlights and see the people you need to release.

Now say to them silently, 'I love you. Thank you for being there for me when I needed you. Please forgive me for wanting to move on from you and I forgive myself for using you as an emotional dumping ground. We are all free now. May you find what you are looking for. Thank you.'

As you finish these words just imagine the people leaving the room and feel how light the atmosphere in there is as a result. As a result of this process, you will feel more empowered and will gain clarity around your own emotions.

Carrying versus caring

At my Awakening events, people frequently tell me, 'This is life changing! I wish my brother were here,' 'I wish my daughter could listen to this,' 'My husband definitely needs this.' My reply, 'Then why are you here?' The same principle goes for life. Be here for you. Work on you. Stop feeling responsible for everyone else's feelings; the Universe does not operate on your shoulders!

We love and care for other people because we are social beings and we are here to create experiences. However, if you are carrying others then you are taking responsibility for their experience and helping them at your own expense. I believe that when you take responsibility for someone else's life you disempower them. The best way to help people is to build them up with love. When you surround people with love, it strengthens them. When you take responsibility for your own life you realize that you don't carry people, you care for them. A healthy relationship should be one where you feel you want to be there because you enjoy the interaction rather than feeling saddled by a sense of responsibility or feeling that you ought to be there for the other person.

If you are concerned for someone's wellbeing, sometimes the best thing to do is to send them love. This way your true intentions will get through to them on an energetic level and they will benefit from the positive energy you are sending out to them. Love is the only transformative feeling that truly heals. Make it a daily habit. Remember, everything is energy and when you are thinking about sending them love, you are sending them love.

Daily Practice: Bubble of love

Use this Daily Practice to help all those people you worry about and feel you are carrying. You can also use it to heal a rift in a relationship that is important to you and is causing you upset. The more often you do this exercise, the easier you will find it to pass on loving energy to others and, this in turn, will help all your relationships.

Make a list in your Awakening journal of all the people you feel are a burden on you.

Start by taking a few breaths and focus on your breathing for a few moments to bring your into the present moment.

Now close your eyes and imagine all of the people surrounded by a glowing iridescent bubble of love.

To those people who burden you
In your mind, say to them: 'I love you enough to care for you and know that you are powerful and able to take care of any challenge that is showing up in your life right now. I release all hooks and attachment from the dependency we have created and with love I let you go. May you become strong and empowered in your own light.

Working on your relationships

As I described earlier (see page 8), all of life is based on relationships; everything connects with everything else. So when your relationship with yourself improves, so will your relationship with everyone around you. You do your deepest work on yourself when you tackle your relationships because this is one area where what you put in is directly reflected back to you. Transforming your own issues shifts your energy blockages and allows new connections to form. This either attracts new people into your life or changes the way you relate to people you currently know.

Whether you decide to work on your relationship with your parents, siblings, lover, children, co-workers or friends, it starts with you: how you decide to interact. It's your decision whether to block the energy, use it to open new channels, or – if you have been carrying instead of caring for someone – decide to let them go. However you decide to conduct the relationship in the future the energy will be reflected and fed back to you.

Forgiveness sets you free

Most of us have probably experienced a situation where we feel that we have been wronged, hurt or treated unjustly by someone close to us. The event leaves a scar in our subconscious that continually and subtly reminds us of the wound, making it difficult for us to move forward or to trust new people. Forgiveness is key here because if you can't forgive all those who have contributed toward that pain then you will keep repeating the situation over and over again until you learn to integrate the lesson it's trying to teach you. The lesson may also be part of a greater plan for your soul that you need to learn in the earth plane (see page 29). Holding on to resentment, guilt, fear and other difficult emotions clouds your judgment and stops you from seeing your current relationship in its true light.

The truth about forgiveness is that it's not for anyone else – it's about you. For me, forgiving means letting go of all those emotions that are stored in my body, which I no longer want to feel in my life. It gives me a sense of responsibility and empowerment regarding my own emotions. All our emotions – negative and positive – belong to us and no one else. We are responsible for them, and it is the emotions, not the other people that hurt us, that impact our lives the most.

Ask yourself: 'How could you benefit from forgiving one person who has wronged you?'

LETTING GO OF NEGATIVITY AND PAIN

Lisa and Michael had a successful business together for two years. When Lisa discovered that Michael had been stealing from the business she felt hurt and deceived by someone she trusted. Later, she met many people who could have taken her business to the next level but because she had been so wounded by the incident she didn't take the risk and felt crippled by her experience. She didn't trust anyone.

Using the Awakening process, Lisa realized that she was not only angry and upset with her partner but also felt stupid and naive to have allowed that to happen to her. There were layers of different emotions at play; when she peeled away one, another even more powerful feeling appeared. It was a complex knot to untangle.

After spending a few weeks working on forgiveness, Lisa sent me the following message, 'I can't thank you enough for helping me heal myself. Forgiving myself was the big one for me. I didn't realize how much negativity I was holding on to and how many different feelings were involved. I feel so much lighter as a result and feel very hopeful regarding my new venture.'

When we learn to forgive, we set ourselves free because we are able to move on from the hurt, into a space of love and compassion for ourselves and the people around us.

Daily Practice: Forgiveness

This powerful and profound process will help you to let go of all the people in the past who no longer serve you in the present. Its effectiveness, however, is dependent on the depth of your hurt and requires frequent and consistent practice to create long-lasting changes in the way you feel about the other person. Over time, your feelings of hurt, anger, sadness and disappointment, not only toward the other person, but also yourself will change and help you to move on from the past.

Start by closing your eyes and taking a few deep breaths. Focus on your breathing to become fully present in your body.

Imagine that you are stepping into a pure white light. Feel the light streaming down through your crown chakra at the top of your head, downward through your body, touching your head, neck, face, stomach and chest, thighs and legs. Give yourself permission to experience this light . . .

Now, breathe it in and feel it envelop you totally. You are completely protected by the light.

Pick the person you want to work on, someone you feel you need to forgive and let go of. Pay attention to which part of your body responds when you think about that person and the hurt they have caused as you may experience an energetic charge in a specific area.

Now, feel that all the energy is leaving your body and forming the shape of the person you are thinking about. Visualize them in front of you and know that it is safe for you to be in front of that person.

Repeat these words out loud, 'I love you. I am sorry that we have got to this stage. Please forgive me. I forgive you. We are both free. I choose to let go of your energy from my space and I retrieve all my energy from yours. Thank you.'

Repeat these words three times and notice how it feels after saying it each time.

Addressing challenging people

Life is all about learning and everything that happens in our life teaches us a lesson in how to become better and stronger than we were before. When we look at life from this point of view, we recognize that the most challenging people in our lives are also the ones that teach us the most.

The Awakening process is about learning to take responsibility for our own feelings and reactions. This can be difficult when we are faced with someone who seems intent on causing us difficulties. But when we accept that we can't change the way they behave but can control our own behaviours, then we can even learn some powerful lessons from them. For example, we may see them act in a certain way and decide never to behave that way, or they have caused us to learn from our direct experience of their actions.

Think about the following scenario for a moment: you have been accused of something you did not do. You can choose to complain about the situation and submit to it or you can see it as a way of learning about how to deal with a whole range of situations: from being able to handle betrayal, to knowing the value of true friends, to dealing with clearing your name, to understanding how helpless others feel when accused of the same thing. You become stronger and wiser as a result of all the conflicting emotions that had you in turmoil.

Think of someone whose challenging behaviour has made you change the course of your life for the better. The powerful emotions they ignited in you forced you to change something – whether you were happy about it or not at the time. But perhaps now you see that other happier circumstances in your life would simply not have existed without you having to act in a certain way.

Often when someone upsets us we get so wrapped up in our own story that we forget that the other person has their own point of view from which they have acted. Ask yourself: What were they trying to achieve by their behaviour?

Daily Practice: Compassion

I have used this exercise many times in my life to help me through challenging times. Whenever I used to feel angry, I would use the following exercise to get perspective on the situation. Think about someone in your life who is challenging and then use the following process to help you to put things back into perspective. It's very simple and truly profound.

Close your eyes, take a few deep breaths to become fully present in your body.

Now, visualize the person you are finding challenging, make sure that you can see the person in sharp focus and can see the expression on their face.

Place all your attention on them and say, 'Just like me, you are seeking happiness in your life. May you receive happiness. Just like me, you have known sadness, loneliness and despair. May you receive pure love. Just like me, you are learning about life. May you receive the wisdom from this experience. Thank you.'

If you use this exercise regularly, you will find that your dealings with your challenging person become easier to deal with, as they begin to reflect the compassion and love back to you.

Addiction to pain

When we spend a lot of time 'helping' our friends by listening to their problems, we sometimes are unwittingly helping to keep them stuck in the same pattern. Our friend may think that we are willing to talk and listen to them when they are sad or upset, and they might even subconsciously decide that they need to be sad or upset to have our attention.

It's like when kids cry. They associate crying with love because when they get upset an adult usually goes to them and gives them a cuddle. So then they deliberately cry to get attention. When they grow up they (hopefully) realize they no longer have to create pain to get love. But subconsciously, many people continue to operate at that level. They get addicted to pain by associating it with receiving love. This runs underneath the conscious awareness of a person when they become addicted to their problems and use them as a way to relate to others and operate in society. I have seen thousands of people come to the Awakening who consciously want to live an Awakened life with more money, more love and health, but subconsciously they are a victim of their emotional injuries and feel afraid that if their problems 'go away' they won't have anything in common with their friends.

Communicating with people in an empowering way helps them to learn that your attention is won without them having to resort to 'crying'. They fear losing the people closest to them as a result of having no common ground, and this is especially true in intimate relationships.

THE THINGS THAT HOLD US BACK

Georgia was an incredibly beautiful and independent woman with a stable career and a great group of single friends. Georgia liked to go out partying and would often end the evening by bitching and complaining about men. Using the Awakening process she released the hurt that had been holding her back from finding a loving relationship and soon after met a man whom she really liked. However, the more time she spent with her date, the less time she had for her friends. Her friends were prickly and sarcastic about it, and would make comments like, 'You have changed' and 'I can't believe you are dumping me for him.' No matter

> what she did, her friends didn't accept the 'new' her. After three months she broke up with her boyfriend and became 'single' again.

In participating in the Awakening process there will inevitably be loss as well as gain but freeing yourself to live your own truth is some of the most valuable Work On You that you can do.

Daily Practice: Release energy hooks

This process is based on the fifth principle, Energy Is Everything, and will help you to release all those people who are stuck in your energies and influence your behaviours without even realizing it.

Close your eyes, take a few deep breaths to become fully present in your body.

Visualize the person or people who are caught in your energy and dependent on you to be a certain way for them.

Now imagine your hand is a brush and use it to sweep over your shoulders and say, 'I release all hooks and attachment from the dependency of others. I let you all go with love, strong and empowered in your own light.'

Personal change creates global transformation

The best thing about the second principle, Work On You, is that by finding happiness within yourself, you are also contributing toward peace and wellbeing on a global level. In my experience, if you feel very strongly about particular issues on a more global level, there is usually something that you personally resonate with that is guiding your interest.

For me, it is issues connected with empowering women. Any news concerning the abuse of women leaves me very upset. One day I heard on the news that a sixteen-year-old girl was buried alive by her family because she had been talking to boys. This incident triggered so many memories from my past when my dad use to beat me if I talked to a boy. Even when a boy gave me attention, it would be my fault.

Realizing the energetic connection, I began to look more carefully at the global issues my clients felt strongly connected to. Many people wanted to put up a fight against bullying because they had been bullied when they were younger. Another client felt deeply connected to children that were going hungry, and on further inspection it turned out that she had frequently gone hungry as a child.

There are millions of incidents happening across the globe on a daily basis. Why do some affect you so strongly and some don't even register? Start by taking note of them because they are signposts to this truth: everything that shows up in your life has a purpose and is giving you an opportunity to work on your own challenges.

What is happening in the world today that disturbs you the most?

Perhaps it's domestic violence? Global warming? Inequality in the workplace? Corporate greed? Bullying? Animal cruelty? What feelings do you experience when you think about this particular issue? Now try to relate this situation to something it reminds you of in your personal life. If you had the power to control this issue, what would you do to solve it?

The good news is that you have the power to help that situation. Use the ABC process (see page 37) to help you integrate the global issue on a personal level and heal the situation as well.

Living in appreciation

Appreciation and gratitude are the keys to living a fulfilled life. What you appreciate, appreciates. But you can't think appreciation or gratitude you have to be it. That's when the true magic happens. Sometimes people come to me and say, 'I've been "doing appreciation" but it's not working for me.' That's usually because they are doing it and not being it. If you want to invite love, be love. If you want to help someone, help yourself.

Daily Practice: Being love

The following exercise is a very powerful technique that will help you to open your heart centre and accept love.

Put your hand over your heart and say to yourself with feeling, 'I love you. I accept you as you are. I commit to you. You are important. Your life counts.' Say it a few times so that you really connect with your heart and express gratitude toward your heart.

Feel your heart radiating love to every cell and fibre in your body. Feel the presence of any emotions in your heart and experience them and lovingly release them. Put your hand down gently and carry on with your day feeling the expansion of your heart.

As I described earlier (see page 87), the only part of our life that we can control is ourselves. Everything begins from the self and within the self. Before we can love ourselves, or anyone else for that matter, we need to open our heart and clear everything that is no longer working for us. Love yourself as you are right now.

If someone or something is making you angry say, 'I love you because you're making me angry,' 'I love you because you're so stubborn,' 'I love the train because it is late.' Just saying 'I love you' raises your energy vibration. So no matter what emotion you're going through, when you put in, 'I love you because . . .', it lifts the vibration. So when you're feeling that you don't love a particular situation, when the train is late, or you've spilled a plate of baked beans on your new carpet or someone is making you angry, see it as a chance to readdress the balance in your energetic frequency. The minute you put love on it, you're coming from a good place, and you'll do a better job of rebalancing your energy from a place of annoyance to somewhere more positive.

Everything happens for a reason, so whatever is making you angry is reminding you to balance your love-o-meter.

Self-acceptance

When you accept and love yourself without feeling you're letting anyone else down, life suddenly becomes easier. You'll find help without asking for it and the right person will show up at the right time. Interacting with other people stops becoming an expectant exchange, where you do me a favour, I do you one back, and instead becomes a game of 'paying it forward': someone does me a favour, I do something nice for someone else. That way there is no obligation between you and the person you've helped or who has helped you. You can give freely without knowing you have burdened someone with having to reciprocate, and when you're the one being treated, you can appreciate it for exactly what it is – a gift of love.

When you finally learn to accept who you really are, you'll be able to untangle your issues without being scared of what you'll discover about yourself. You'll finally be able to face your 'unacceptable' truths. The compassion you are now showing yourself allows you to integrate fragments of your character that you had perhaps denied (see the exercise on reintegrating fragments on page 37). Now that you can forgive yourself you will see that you acted in the only way you could at the time to protect yourself or to make yourself feel better.

ACTIVATING THE SECOND PRINCIPLE: WORK ON YOU

In the second step of the Awakening journey, Work On You, one of the most important things we discover is that there is a reason for everything; whether we know it or not at the time. When you work on you, you live your truth; and by loving and self-respecting yourself you extend the same feelings to your friends, family, colleagues and the world. Practising compassion, forgiveness and acceptance you remain open to the experience of every situation you encounter and this can help you to live your best life possible. All that you do, you do for yourself. What you do for another, you do for you. What is good for another is good for you. You are a human being – what you are being is decided by you.

In the next principle, Awareness Is The Key, we'll explore values, beliefs and behaviours in more depth and discover ways to transform those parts of your life that are outdated and keeping you stuck.

Divine Magic Statement

I am willing to disappoint another to be true to myself. I love, accept and approve of myself in totality.

Awareness Is The Key

'*No problem can be solved from the same level of consciousness that created it.*'

Albert Einstein

Your awareness is your reality; it is everything you know. This third principle, Awareness Is The Key, is the next truth to absorb on your Awakening journey. Expanding your awareness, and therefore your consciousness, will bring you closer to your own truth. Your awareness determines how you show up in life: whether you fulfil your purpose in life or don't. The truth of who we really are is usually hidden beneath our conditioning and programming, so we need to spend some time infusing it with energy that is more aligned with our true self. In other words, you might think you are a businessperson just like your dad, but deep down inside there is a musician that hasn't been given an opportunity to shine yet.

Conscious living

When you delve beneath the surface and look at what's really going on, the things you did before out of habit, you will now do out of choice. When you become truly aware of what you're doing and why, you have a choice to follow through with that action or pick a different one. You can't be what you are not aware of, and you may even spend your entire life being what you are not!

THE EAGLE IN THE FARMYARD

There was once a farmer who diligently worked his land, day in, day out. It was a hard and lonely life. One fine day he was seized by a desire to climb the mountain that overshadowed his farm and see what he could see. So he downed tools and began to climb. Up, up, up he went. As he pulled himself onto a ledge just below the summit, his hand brushed a pile of twigs. A nest – and it was full of eggs! He knew at once that they were eagle's eggs. Delighted at his find, he very gently took one of the eggs and carried it all the way back down the mountain to his farm. For safekeeping he put the egg under one of his hens, who happened to be sitting on a clutch of eggs.

The mother hen was proud of this egg that was so much larger than any other egg on the farm and she looked after it as if it had been her own. In due course the egg cracked open and an eagle chick emerged. Even as a baby, the eagle had the piercing eyes and proud beak of its kind. It looked quite different to the fluffy yellow chicks, but the kind farm animals had no fear of this magnificent creature and the little eagle was treated just like all the chickens. Its foster mother taught it all about the farm's pecking order, and showed it how to cluck and scratch.

The eagle grew old believing itself to be a chicken. Then one day, as it was pulling a worm out of the earth, a shadow fell over the ground and the eagle looked up. High above, a majestic eagle soared, gliding effortlessly on the wind. 'What a wonderful creature!' exclaimed the eagle. Never in all his life had he seen anything so regal and graceful.

'Just keep digging,' said a hen. 'Those eagles don't have anything to do with us. We're only chickens and our wings are for taking dust baths, not flying.'

Hearing that, the eagle took his eyes off the soaring bird and turned his attention back to the dusty farmyard. He believed himself to be a chicken – and that's all he would ever be.

Just like the old eagle in the story above, we decide whether to continue behaving in a certain way or not, whether to think differently or to react in a particular manner. And if we still decide to act in the way we did before, we do it with full awareness. This is conscious living.

Knowing why you do something makes you responsible for your choices and means any repressed or subconscious feelings will no longer pop up and hijack your intentions or your behaviours. Things that were previously invisible, unavailable or that you just did not know about will become obvious. So if you have been struggling with a particular issue but have no idea why, expanding your awareness of what's happening on a deeper level will bring other matters to the fore. Perhaps you'll realize that your issues don't actually belong to you but are an echo of another family member's feelings on the subject. You might discover that you have fear or guilt issues around it. For example, people who experienced scarcity in childhood often subconsciously feel ashamed or unable to enjoy their success because they remember the pain money caused their parents.

OLD ANXIETY AROUND MONEY

During a very cold winter David, a very wealthy man in his eighties, was found unconscious is his unheated house suffering from hypothermia. After he was hospitalized his daughter, Maria, was very worried about him and pleaded with him to spend some money on heating. When he ignored her wishes Maria knew her father was deep in denial about how close he had come to losing his life and persuaded her father to come and see me.

David described how when he was a young boy during World War II his father was killed in battle overseas and his mother was left to bring up David and his two brothers on a meagre widow's pension. Although David remembered little of his childhood, he always felt very close to his mother and respected her immensely for managing to bring up the family in such harsh conditions. He said nothing was ever wasted in their house. Everything was used until it fell to bits. His mother was incredibly resourceful and hated seeing anything go to waste.

He vowed to himself that he would never live like that again and consequently became a huge success in the printing industry. Deep down he hoped his success would make his mother feel better. He tried to make her accept some gifts but she found it difficult, saying he shouldn't 'waste' his money on her. He was a rich man but couldn't enjoy a penny he earned. Despite losing his mother nearly 40 years before, he continued to carry her feelings about scarcity into his old age.

A couple of months after his session, Maria got in touch to say that her father had decided to take her

> and his granddaughter on a trip of a lifetime, to enjoy some of his money while he was still fit and able. She said that after our meeting he had grieved for his mother properly for the first time. He had been holding onto the money as tightly as he could because letting go meant letting go of her. But now he felt strong enough to stop punishing himself and live his last few years truly enjoying the fruits of what he had worked so hard for all his life.

Many children who are raised in a poor economic environment inherit their parents' fears of lack of abundance or resources. I've met hoarders whose houses were so filled with junk that they couldn't find their beds. Once they become aware that their fear of scarcity was handed down from their parents, they were finally able to make space for themselves. I have also met people who cannot bear to let go of anything because they are living out their unexpressed grief and have never truly let go of the person they lost.

We make decisions about life based on the information we have at the time. To help you understand the third principle of Awakening more fully, imagine three people looking at the same garden. The first person sees the plants, the soil and flowers and knows that it requires sun, water and nourishment to grow. The second person sees the garden and knows what it takes to grow plus the medicinal qualities of each of the plants. The third person knows all of the above but also that each plant has its own consciousness and that they are all connected to everything else. This knowing is a real understanding. His understanding of the garden is more powerful than just knowing about what the plants need and use.

*In becoming aware, we receive more information
about a situation, and so can make informed decisions.*

Beliefs

If something in your life is not functioning properly, the chances are you have a belief around that issue that needs updating. You're probably not even yet aware that you're caught up in a negative, repetitive pattern, but if you're caught up in a chaotic cycle with bad relationship after bad relationship, difficult boss after difficult boss, or even with baffling health issues, then you're probably operating subconsciously on that issue. You need more information so that you can resolve the conflict or you will keep playing the record over and over until you understand it: you don't know what you don't know.

I didn't know that all the problems I was having with my ex-husband were actually issues I was having with myself. They were really about things that happened in my past but because I had no awareness of the anxiety I had around my dad, and with men in general, I projected my messed-up stuff onto my husband. It was only by immersing myself deeply in personal development work that I expanded my awareness and understood that my problems really weren't with my husband – he was just a representation of my past. The problem was with my beliefs about men.

A moment of clarity came to me when I was ice-skating. For the eighth or ninth time I fell on exactly the same spot. I was really tired and fed up, the same way I'd been feeling about my marriage. No matter how hard I tried I couldn't make it work. I stared at the ice rink and saw there was a little mound of ice that kept tripping me up on the very same spot I'd be falling on. I thought of how my husband and I kept fighting about the same issues all the time, neither of us were aware of the little ice mound that had been triggering our problem.

In my life, that ice mound symbolized the belief that I had formed around relationships, which was tripping me up every time we hit conflict. I worked out that my belief was, 'Marriage is about two people sharing one life', and that made me needy for my husband's time and attention. His belief was, 'Marriage is about two independent people sharing experiences when they want to.' My belief was the result of the environment I grew up in and so was his. Neither of us was right nor wrong, we were just different. Looking at my problem and thinking about it in a different way brought new information and expanded my knowledge and awareness around it.

Awareness helps us go beneath the surface and identify where the real conflict is coming from.

Uncovering beliefs

When we have believed something for a long time, we have an emotional attachment to that belief. The precise nature of your beliefs will be individual but you might, for example, believe the following:

- Life is a struggle.
- Money doesn't grow on trees.
- Relationships don't last forever.
- All women are selfish.
- All men are chauvinistic.

The list is endless but the one thing all beliefs have in common is that they are subconsciously comfortable and keep giving us the same experiences that we believe to be true.

UNCOVERING BELIEFS

Pam was a high-profile investment banker. She and her partner had been trying for a baby but nothing seemed to be happening. After exploring all the conventional routes she decided to come along to one of my live Awakening events. Using the 'Becoming aware of your beliefs' and 'Identifying beliefs' (see opposite and page 106) Daily Practices, she discovered one of her core beliefs.

Pam's mother had had to leave her job in order to look after Pam and she often heard her mother complaining about how having Pam had ruined her career. Pam grew up believing that, 'Having kids ruins your career.' She loved her job but had unconsciously decided that raising a family would be in direct conflict with her ambitions. Using the ABC process (see page 37) she was able to release that belief and create a new idea that, 'Having kids will add to my résumé as a person and gives me a choice to expand my working life.' Later, she informed me that she had become a proud mother of a wonderful daughter.

Resolving conflict

The way to resolve conflict between our conscious and subconscious beliefs is first to identify the conflict and take responsibility for its energy in our life. Somewhere down the line we made a decision about how we felt about a particular aspect of our lives and now live according to that decision. We must respect that our subconscious doesn't know that the decision we made years ago is holding us back.

Daily Practice: Becoming aware of your beliefs

If you recognize that a belief is holding you back and you want to overcome it then first you must reason with your subconscious by communicating with it. You can uncover your beliefs by asking your subconscious for specifics by using the following quality questions and recording your answers in your Awakening journal.

For example, you might ask:

- Who did I see struggling in life and why?
- What is it about making money that stops me from making it.
- What exactly is it about being in a loving relationship that scares me?
- Which men or women in my life affected my thinking about 'all men' or 'all women'?

Give yourself time for a response to come. Answers such as, 'I don't want to sacrifice my freedom', or 'I don't want to be responsible for someone else's feelings' might come up. Take some time to appreciate the answers; they are your true feelings.

Then you can start to reason with your subconscious. For example, you might say, 'If my freedom gets compromised, I'll leave,' or 'Everyone is responsible for their own feelings.' Keep reasoning with yourself. Maybe even come up with some examples of people who have achieved what you want to achieve.

You can only change the energy of your beliefs when you are prepared to address old patterns so keep at it, coax it out, and then you will find that there was nothing to be frightened of.

We all have certain core beliefs that sum up our view of life. If you believe that 'life is hard', 'people are selfish', or that 'change is difficult', then it will be. If you have decided to believe something is true, then that's exactly what life will be for you. On the other hand, if you believe 'life is fun', 'people are kind', or 'change is an adventure', then you will meet your beliefs in the form of attracting kind people and exciting situations. You don't even have to be aware of your beliefs to be able to change them, as one of the most effective ways to explore your beliefs is to look at different areas of life and think about how you really feel about them.

Daily Practice: Identifying beliefs

Set aside some time and keep your Awakening journal to hand so that you can jot down your ideas.

Start by choosing an area of your life in which you wish to explore your beliefs. For example, it might be relationships, money, love, health, success, your body, religion, luck or happiness. Write down everything that springs to mind on that topic. Try not to censor your thoughts; just let them spill out onto the page. When you're done, read what you've written and examine how true these thoughts and feelings are in comparison to how your life is right now.

Now ask yourself:

- 'Do your beliefs reflect the situation you are facing?'
- 'Is there any conflict in what you believe or any situation in your life that you would like to change?'

Now use the ABC process (see page 37) for each old belief that you want to release and transform to suit your current life.

Attracting love into your life

If you haven't been in a relationship for a while, but would like to meet someone, making yourself aware of anything that's holding you back and processing it will open you up to meeting new people and attracting love into your life. It's likely that you are operating subconsciously and playing out someone else's programs or holding onto a belief about relationships that isn't even yours.

Most of us were imprinted with the relationship that our parents had with each other. It's difficult not to absorb their energy when we're little because we see our parents as gods. They have complete power over our lives and when we are small we have no concept of our parents being wrong or even different to other people. They are our archetypal blueprints for relationships. Think about your parents' marriage and how that has impacted you. Ask yourself:

- How did your mother and father relate to each other when you were younger?
- Was it an equal, balanced partnership?
- Did one parent dish out the discipline?
- What were you parents' grievances with each other?
- Did they put on a show where they were happy to outsiders but in private it was a different story?

Try to recall any arguments or difficult times and feel how you might have been programmed with their view of love or partnership. Even the happiest marriages have their ups and downs. If you were brought up by a single parent, spend some time feeling what that experience has taught you, or if you lost a parent when you were young, think about what emotions that brings up for you now, as you think about meeting someone new. For example, during a workshop one of the participants used the following exercise and had a major realization about why he was twice divorced. The sentence he was given to complete was, 'To be happy with one person for the rest of my life is a concept . . . ' and his answer was 'I find extremely boring.' His boredom in the relationship was the issue in both marriages but he didn't know it until that moment!

Daily Practice: Love beliefs

If you can't remember much about your parents consciously, this exercise will bring up areas that you need to explore in more depth.

Complete the following sentences spontaneously – this will give you awareness of your underlying beliefs about relationships. Be aware of the actual words you use because the ones that spring to mind first will give you precious clues about what's really going on at a subconscious level with your beliefs. Try not to over analyze what comes up: you don't want your conscious mind getting too involved in this process.

- All women/men are . . .
- When it comes to love I always . . .
- I tend to meet suitors who are . . .
- When I'm good to people . . .
- If I show my feelings I am . . .
- When I think of love I feel . . .
- To be happy with one person for the rest of my life is a concept . . .
- If I meet my perfect partner I am afraid . . .
- Love is . . .

Don't be surprised if you get answers you weren't expecting, but think about it further and look carefully at your current situation. It is likely that you'll find that your statements are actually being reflected in your relationships.

Once you have revealed your core beliefs, you can use ABC process (see page 37) to replace the old beliefs with the news ones that are more aligned with your current life.

Make sure you keep your mantra grounded in the present tense. What you believe, is, so don't say 'I can live an exciting life' say, 'I am living an exciting life.' Try these or come up with your own tailored mantras.

- Old belief: I can never be happy.
- New belief: I am happy and my happiness lasts.
- Old belief: I never have enough money.
- New belief: I always have enough money / I am looked after.
- Old belief: My childhood messed me up.
- New belief: My childhood gave me wisdom.

Ancient beliefs

Once you start to become aware of some of the beliefs that are running in the background of your life, you need to evaluate which ones are still true for you and which ones are unhelpful or tripping you up and go about changing their energy into something that is more aligned with your current life. The first step in this process is to start tracing back to find the belief's creation.

COLLAPSING BELIEFS

Jack was in a financially viable business, but no matter what he did and no matter how hard he worked, he wasn't able to increase his salary. By asking quality questions, we came across his core belief around money, 'I must not be successful.' By working with guided meditations we uncovered that Jack's core beliefs were supported by many events that had happened in the past.

He grew up in a working-class family where his father left his mother to work abroad. All Jack heard from his mother was how 'money took my husband away' and that 'successful people are selfish', which created an association of pain with success as he saw his mother in pain, as a result of his father being successful.

After clearing the childhood trauma, his financial situation got better, he started closing more deals but he was still unable to retain the money that he was beginning to earn.

In the next session, we used regression therapy to go deeper and he came across a memory from the early 1800s. He had inherited a great deal of money but was being very cruel to people around him and not using it to make his friends' or family's situation any better. We used the ABC process (see page 37) to release the guilt around him for abusing his power.

In later sessions, we discovered that it was his mother's experience of money in her childhood that had given him the invisible upper limit of how much he could earn. After six months of consistently working on his money issue Jack now earns more in one month than his previous annual income.

Our beliefs are usually formed in our current timeline, as a result of an experience, as in Pam or David's case, or the belief has been passed on through the ancestral timeline. In my experience beliefs are like tables with many legs. Each leg represents a different facet of that core belief. If you want to collapse the table, then you have to remove each of the legs in turn so that the table collapses; the same applies to the belief.

Daily Practice: Time travel tunnels

If you want to get in touch more deeply with the beliefs that were formed in your current timeline then this guided meditation will help you. Used regularly, this practice can also help you intuit the deep-seated beliefs that are held in your superconscious and formed in your ancestral and eternal timelines.

Choose a quiet place and a time when you'll be undisturbed. Read through the exercise a few times so you are familiar with the steps before beginning. The key to self-guided meditation is to make your visualizations as real and lifelike as possible so that you experience it with all your senses.

Now, take a few deep breaths. Focus on your breath to help quiet your mind and bring your attention to the present moment. Spend a few moments relaxing deeply.

Imagine that you are walking through a forest. Feel your feet crunch on leaves on the ground, hear the birds, smell the scent of the flowers and trees around you. Enjoy the fresh air.

Soon you find yourself at the mouth of a cave. This is a very special place and you can see different passageways in front of you. Torches of fire light each passageway.

Think of the belief you wish to change the most: the one that's been holding you back in life. With your fullest intention, ask yourself: 'If this belief could live in my body, where would I sense it?

Connect with the energy of that belief by feeling its presence in your body. Take your attention and awareness to that part of your body and focus on that belief.

Now, look at those passageways – one holds the origin of your belief. Feel which one calls you toward it and walk down the tunnel – you are travelling through time.

At the end of that passageway is the event that formed your belief. You might see or sense the event itself or experience something else. Pay attention to your emotions and physical responses, as well as the images, sounds or smells you pick up. (Even if you don't sense anything this still works on a subconscious and superconscious level.)

Now, say the following, 'I give thanks to all those who contributed toward the formation of this belief. I lovingly release all files, patterns, attachments, indulgences and programs related to this belief that can be cleared. I now freely choose to allow the old belief of [*state the belief*] to be replaced and integrated with the new belief of [*state the new, positive statement*].

When you feel you have completed your journey, slowly bring yourself back to the present.

Clear your mental chatter to resolve inner conflict

Quieting your mind is not an easy task in today's world with our dependence on technology. We are easily distracted and sometimes we prefer it that way. Often we are actually trying to avoid connecting with ourselves for fear of what we might discover. But if you want to be able to see what's inside, you need to turn the outside 'down' a few notches so that you can check in with yourself.

When we take the time to really experience what we're actually like without all the input from our environment –

work, family, friends and relationships – we become more able to drive ourselves toward situations that are best for the growth of our soul.

Daily Practice: Silencing the noise

This is a wonderful meditation when you need to unplug from life and just be.

Choose a quiet place and a time when you'll be undisturbed. Read through the exercise a few times so you are familiar with the steps before beginning.

Take a few deep breaths in and out, and focus on your breath for a few moments to bring your mind and body into the present moment.

Imagine you are standing under a sparkling waterfall of light. This waterfall is cleansing your energy. As the water runs from your head all the way down to the tips of your toes, it cleanses your body of all the emotions that are the result of conflict between your inner voices and lets them wash away in the glistening water.

Imagine that your mind has a huge central control system. On the left there is a switchboard that has a sign saying 'external noise'. Go there and press the 'off' button. Look around and find the button that says 'mental clutter' and press 'off'.

Start to become aware of the transformation occurring within you. If unnecessary thoughts intrude, acknowledge them and then dismiss them.

Allow yourself to become aware of the presence of silence. The sense of serenity is filling every nerve, every fibre and cell in your body. Feel this silence spreading throughout every layer and level of your being. Enjoy this experience for as long as you are drawn to it.

Recognizing your inner voices

When we learn to quiet our mind we become more aware of the little voice in our head. If you are wondering 'What voice?' then that is the exact voice I am talking about – the one that asked, 'What voice?' It is the voice that usually fills you with fear, doubts and anxiety and since you are not aware of it, most of the time you end up feeling all of those emotions without knowing why.

This is your 'ego' speaking and its purpose is to help you function in society. It is the limited, separated, illusory self, which cannot see beyond its own purpose. It lives off the fear that we might not get what we want and drives us to satisfy our human needs. It's the ego that nags us to get a better house, better job or to look more beautiful. In fact, it's the ego that pushes us out of bed to do anything!

Ask, 'Who is speaking?'

Your task is to understand your ego by becoming aware of the source of your behaviours. If you are unaware of the ego then it plays out in different forms: fear, sabotage, judgment, jealousy, guilt – all these emotions are the result of ego running a program in the back of our minds that makes us feel these feelings.

Resolving inner conflict

Transactional analysis is a psychological theory that sees the ego as having three major voices that dictate our lives. These are:

The Child: The voice that demands freedom, adventure and excitement.

The Adult: A rational, logical voice that makes us go to work even when we don't want to and meet our obligations.

The Parent: A critical, judgmental voice that keeps saying, 'You are not good enough,' 'Do better than this.'

These inner voices are like children in the classroom. If the children are talking and fighting with each other then they won't learn anything and progress. In order to create a life of wisdom and integrate the lessons that we sign up for then it is important to become aware of these voices and learn to communicate with them. This will result in harmony and balance in the classroom of life and the lesson will be learned with ease and grace.

Daily Practice: Journalling

I invite you to become an observer of your own life. Just passively observe your beliefs, thoughts, emotions, inner voices and behaviours. Just become aware of it all.

Look at yourself going through the motions of life. Keeping a journal of what you notice will show you that everything is connected. Note when you hear the Child speaking, and what obligations your Adult voice keeps telling you you must do, and when you hear the Parent criticizing you. The Universe is always giving us a shove in the right direction to help us learn what we need to evolve.

Remembering your dreams can give you tremendous insight into your inner world, as they are a direct link to what's happening in your subconscious. Often just the act of writing down a dream can have a magical effect. When you look into the detail of a moment in your dream it can peel back a whole layer of other dream imagery that you had since forgotten.

Consciously we all want a life full of health, wealth and happiness but we still end up making decisions that are not good for us. We know that regular exercise and eating healthily is beneficial for us and still we end up sitting in front of television eating junk. What is it in us that persuades us to hang on to toxic relationships when we know that we deserve better? We might even fall into the trap of comparison and start to consider ourselves as 'weak minded'. The truth is that when we are aware of how our ego is creating the conflict we can take steps to resolve the inner conflict.

Daily Practice: Befriend your ego

In this process, you are going to go within and meet your ego. Remember that your ego is your manager and wants to look after your needs as an individual. By connecting and communicating with it, you are updating the cellular memory of that program.

Choose a quiet place and a time when you'll be undisturbed. Read through the exercise a few times so you are familiar with the steps before beginning. The key to self-guided meditation is to make your visualizations as real and lifelike as possible so that you experience it with all your senses.

Take a few deep breaths and focus on your breathing to become fully present in your body.

Imagine you are walking through a beautiful forest. The ground beneath your feet is soft and the sun is shining, gently warming your skin. Listen to the sounds of nature all around you.

Notice that you are on a path; follow it wherever it leads.

Soon the path leads to a clearing in the trees where there is a majestic oak tree. Rest your back against that tree; it is here that you will meet your ego.

Connect with the consciousness of your body and ask your ego to reveal itself. Connect with the presence of the ego in your body then allow it to leave and stand in front of you. It may take the form of a person, creature or any other object.

Say 'hello' to your ego in a friendly way.

Now say, 'Thank you for protecting me and helping me. I am now connected to the greatest wisdom that is present to me each moment. I acknowledge you for all the roles you have shown up as in my life. I am 100 percent committed and willing to integrate all those parts of me that I am unaware of. Please show me all those aspects of me that are playing out in different guises. Thank you.'

Be patient and allow your ego to reveal all those facets of yourself. You might see or sense an event, people, emotions or just a blank space.

When you are aware of the roles your ego has played, say 'I release, remove and clear all traumatic memories that have been recorded in my cellular memory at all levels, due to my lack of awareness of my ego. I welcome all these aspects of me with love and awareness. I integrate and align them all with my intention to live an Awakened life with love, compassion, truth and grace. Thank you.'

Gifts of awareness

Awakening brings gifts of awareness and suddenly routine events that perhaps you never paid attention to before come alive because you appreciate them in a new light. The sense of wonder you have been conditioned to stifle with layers of programming will slowly rise to the surface of your life again and colour your outlook with fresh possibilities.

When you shift your awareness, even on a small scale, you will notice that events in your life appear to be more 'connected' than they were before. That's because you're more in tune with the bigger picture, you're seeing how you're plugged into the vast energy matrix of consciousness.

Things happen in an intricate plan that is usually beyond our conscious awareness. But when you start paying attention to what's happening around you, you will learn that the Universe is continually giving you messages, sometimes very obvious ones. These don't have to be 'mystical' or 'overwhelming', they could be simple little things that appear out of the blue, little acts of synchronicity such as seeing a heart-shaped cloud or hearing someone's name who's important to you. You will begin to see the sacred in the mundane and the mundane in the sacred.

> *Appreciate the beauty in your life by not only becoming aware of it but also by learning to express it too.*

Daily Practice: Appreciation challenge

Keeping a gratitude list is a lovely way to reconnect with the here and now.

Start by writing down five things that you appreciate in this very moment, and if you can't think of any just write, 'I appreciate that I am here', or 'I appreciate that I am in a body that works', 'That I have enough food', 'That I have a roof over my head', 'That I am safe'. There is always something to appreciate.

By truly living your life with conscious awareness you will experience moments of pure joy. When you can see through the games your ego plays and understand that everybody is here for a spiritual experience, you will feel connected once again to the Source.

ACTIVATING THE THIRD PRINCIPLE: AWARENESS IS THE KEY

In the third step of the Awakening journey, Awareness Is The Key, we realize how, when we take time out to truly become aware of our emotions, behaviours and beliefs, we are in the best place to deal with them and shift their energy into something more positive. The same goes for thoughts. They are energetic thought forms that are continually moving, reforming and changing. So once you are aware of how you show up in life, you can control where you would like to go next.

In the next principle, Knowing Versus Owning, we'll explore overcoming fear and the power that comes from surrendering to the unknown.

Divine Magic Statement

I am committed and willing to see the truth of who I am. It is safe for me to make the unknown.

Knowing Versus Owning

'Visualization without action is delusion. No tools in the world can turn your wood into a table unless you pick them up and use them.'

Sidra Jafri

On your journey to becoming an Awakened being, the fourth principle, Knowing Versus Owning, serves to remind us that the noblest feeling we can experience is wonder at life's mysteries. Children are entranced by the simplest of things, water running over pebbles or the progress of ants across a path. To open up to the miracles of life we must once more surrender to the unknown. Part of this process is feeling safe in the knowledge that the Universe has our back while we overcome our fears and discover our truth. On a spiritual level, you probably already know the answers to the truths you are seeking, and the fourth principle will prompt you to explore other paths and perhaps speed up your evolutionary voyage.

Acknowledging the vacuum

There was something missing in my life. I was seeing clients on a regular basis as a practising hypnotherapist and still attending self-development courses and discovering new techniques and ideas. But something wasn't right with me and I felt troubled because I couldn't work out what it was. On the surface I was doing everything right.

What started out as a vague feeling of dissatisfaction grew until I could no longer ignore it. Getting to the bottom of the issue took a while but I did my best to approach the problem with an inquiring heart . . . and then when working on opening myself to new possibilities I realized I had hit the truth: I knew it all but I wasn't owning it!

I was preaching the tools of self-help and self-awareness but I wasn't actually using them to make myself better. I was still very unhappy in my marriage but for some reason I wasn't using my knowledge to help myself heal. So why wasn't I practising what I preached? After all, I believed in it and understood why it worked so why had I been avoiding using my insightful wisdom on myself? Deep down I knew the answer and I didn't like it: fear.

I had already acted courageously to get my life to where it was and didn't want to admit that I still had more work to do. I was scared and my conscious mind was not happy to admit it. After all, fear was something I assumed I had already conquered and won! I thought I was on the road to self-discovery and happiness, and that I was teaching others to do the same. But actually I wasn't really on the road at all.

Sometimes we sit on the road, looking at the road ahead, too frightened of what might happen if we joined the traffic.

Overcoming fear

Fear is primal. It exists to protect us from losing the things that make us feel secure. In the night when we hear a noise we can't identify, fear makes sure we are alert and ready for action. It's the emotion that reminds us what happened the last time we met an angry dog or crossed the road without looking.

Fear has probably saved your life by keeping you away from the edge of 30th floor or made you drive cautiously on an icy road. Those are examples of healthy, rational fears. But there is another type of fear that lives inside your mind like a gremlin. It makes your heartbeat go crazy when you think about speaking in public or causes your mouth to go dry when you ask for the pay rise you are due.

I once heard someone describe fear as 'False Evidence Appearing Real'. If you think there is a thief outside who's waiting to attack you, regardless of whether there's actually somebody out there or not, your body will respond with fear. You can think yourself into a fearful state. Fear cannot differentiate between what is real and what is not. It views all ventures outside of your comfort zone as a possible hazard. Irrational fear is created by the illusion of separation. It lives in a dark, disconnected place where you are no longer connected with the Source; where you don't feel good enough, powerful enough or deserving enough to create the life you truly desire. Like our beliefs, there are countless fears but the most common ones – fear of failure, success, judgment, rejection or abandonment – are all interlinked and at their core they all have one dread – change.

- Fear of failure wants you to believe, 'There's no point in making an effort as you will never succeed.'
- Fear of success dictates that,'If things change, then people will feel uncomfortable around you.'
- Fear of judgment likes to remind us that, 'If you do that, what will people think?'
- Fear of rejection yells. 'If you act like that, you will be denied.'
- Fear of abandonment convinces us that, 'If you change, people will leave you and you will be alone.'

The best way to address our fears is to first understand that it comes from the ego and is only doing its job: protecting us from the unknown. Intense irrational fears can be crippling and even hinder our day-to-day life but usually have a point of creation that we can pinpoint to help us break through the obstruction it has created. There is usually a good reason why the fear developed in the first place, even though it's no longer helping us in our current timeline, as the following story demonstrates.

PHOBIA OF ANTS

Jo came to me because she wanted to work on her fear of ants. She was 36 and a mother of a young boy. She couldn't understand why she was so afraid of ants but it stopped her from going into the garden. Just the thought of them brought shivers to her spine. When we explored her past we were able to connect with Jo as a young frightened little girl, and Jo talked about the movie *Ants* in which there were ants that ate people. In her young mind, there was no difference between watching a movie and what happened in real life and nobody had explained to her that the movie wasn't real. Ants ate people! So obviously they would want to eat her too. When Jo was able to identify the point of creation and shed the light of awareness to that echo, the fear simply vanished.

I am always amazed by how simple, yet profound, these processes can be. All we have to do is to access the fear that is stored within our psyche and remove the program that created the obstacle. One of the major interferences preventing people accessing fear is denial: it is the enemy of change. 'But I am not in denial,' I hear you think, but what you are experiencing is denial of denial, which keeps your friend fear protected in the subconscious so that you don't even know it exists.

Denial, fear's right-hand guy, had happily crept in to save me from uncovering any more painful or uncomfortable feelings. So I wasn't even aware that I was fearful of dealing with my unhappy marriage. I just wasn't going there emotionally because I knew it would hurt. Nobody finds facing his or her personal demons easy! But not dealing with your real feelings distracts you from really evolving and uncovering your true identity.

Sometimes we are so attached to our problems that we think we are those problems. The anxieties themselves become part of who we are and we become unable to imagine ourselves without them.

The face changes but energy remains

When we deny emotional pain it always comes back in some other form. The pain is true and must be acknowledged so that its lesson can be integrated and we can move forward and really evolve. Pain's role is to alert us to something being wrong so we can heal it and move on. But admitting to the pain means experiencing it all over again, and that's not usually something we consciously want to take on. When we try to ignore our issues, we often find that the same lesson keeps popping back in different guises until we are able to confront it.

TAKING CONTROL

When he was 12 years old Jamie and his uncle were involved in a traumatic accident involving three other vehicles. Another driver lost control of his car and two people died in the resulting pile-up. Incredibly,

Jamie and his uncle were unharmed, physically, but deeply traumatized by the accident. They were both given counselling for a few months after the event and managed to put it behind them.

Jamie came to see me when he was in his late thirties and a successful hotelier. Outwardly he was the epitome of a well-adjusted, popular man with a successful career. But he had been having problems adjusting to family life. He had two young sons and was obsessed about their welfare and found himself trying to control their every move. Over the years he had become obsessed with managing everyone he was close to, including his wife and colleagues.

When I asked him about his life when he was younger he mentioned the car accident but said 'that had all been dealt with'. I wondered if Jamie had come to terms with the accident on an intellectual level but hadn't released the emotions. When I asked him why he wanted to be in charge of everyone he said, it was 'out of protection', because if something bad happened he would want to be able to 'steer them out of trouble'. In fact, he used a few driving terms; 'steer', 'take the wheel,' and even asked what I was 'driving at'.

We discussed whether the words he was using were still linking him with the accident and that's when he let go of all the anguished feelings he had been trying to avoid for 20 years. He said he had talked about the accident many times previously but had never emotionally connected with what had happened. The trauma had created anxiety that had permeated many areas of his life. In the accident he felt out of control because his life was in his uncle's hands, and even he had no control of what was happening. Jamie made a subconscious decision then to never be in a situation like that again. So without realizing it, Jamie decided to control everyone around him for their own protection. It took him months to clear away all the traumas and eventually be free.

Most of us have experienced events that have installed fear in our minds and until we break through denial, we won't get anywhere. Even if we are consciously embracing change, if our subconscious has issues with fear we'll come up with an excuse to stay just as we are. Sometimes our mind will deny there's anything wrong, and we'll hear our internal voice saying, 'Oh that doesn't apply to me' or 'I'm fine on that front'. But the fact that the situation showed up in our life means there is something in us that requires attention.

Recognizing what is truly happening in your life can sometimes be difficult because owning up to the issues will inevitably make you feel vulnerable, uncomfortable or scared. It takes honesty and courage to admit why things are not the way you want them to be and it's often far easier to repress your feelings than open them up to public view. But remember that denial means we don't recognize what is. We are only fooling ourselves. We are allowing ourselves to believe a different reality and that can only lead to confusion. Denial prevents us getting to the real cause of the issue while creating a false sense of control over the problem.

If you don't own the issue and act upon it, your denial just serves as a chimera – a fantasy that's obscuring the key to your freedom.

Recognizing self-sabotage

When denial and fear get together they spawn self-sabotage. It is another of change's archenemies and does its level best to prevent you from reaching your long-held dreams. We engage in self-sabotage for many reasons. For example, you might be used to failing and, out of habit, find it easier to screw things up rather than admitting you need to try something new. Or deep down you might not feel you fully deserve to make positive changes in your life. Sometimes we self-sabotage to fool ourselves into thinking we have control, such as splitting up with someone we love because we're terrified they might do the same to us. If you get in there first, you'll be better prepared and you imagine you will have more control of the outcome. Of course, you don't because you only broke up with them in the fear that they would abandon you . . . and now you have abandoned yourself!

We don't consciously want to self-sabotage, which explains why sometimes we are genuinely puzzled as to why we acted in a particular way and might say, 'Why did I do that?' or 'Why did I say that?' Other common forms of self-sabotage are:

- Being late for appointments.
- Missing interviews.
- Getting ill on an important day.
- Comfort eating when you have a weight concern.
- Self-harming.

But we also do it when we deliberately anger or offend someone who was helping us to make a change, or when we flunk an exam or task just to prove that we're not capable or worthy of success.

Fear and denial will discover countless, ingenious methods to stop us from changing.

We aren't always aware of this behaviour as being detrimental because there's usually a feeling of comfort associated with the self-sabotage: a feeling of relief that you don't have to deal with something, otherwise you wouldn't do it at all. But staring your demon square in the face is the only way to break the pattern.

FINDING MOTIVATION

Sara was a successful marketer but something was stopping her from going to the next level in her career. She had all the resources to take her business up a few notches but 'didn't know' why she wasn't taking any action.

When she came to see me it quickly became clear that she had been in an unhappy marriage for the last 27 years. Her husband was cheating on her and stealing money from her. Deep down she was asking herself, 'What is the point of earning more money, if he's going to steal it?' The truth was so painful to admit that she chose to remain thinking, 'I don't know what to do'.

It took several sessions before Sara was convinced that her relationship with her husband had anything to with her career. Finally, we carried out an, 'alternate future' where she progressed forward in time to see what her life would look like then. She finally saw that if nothing changed in her marriage, nothing would change in her business, either. Later she admitted that she 'knew' her relationship wasn't working but for the sake of children and her family, she didn't want to address it. She put all her focus on work to keep herself distracted and 'hoped' it would resolve itself. Once Sara became honest with herself, she realized that addressing her marriage was the only way she could move forward.

The most common answer I hear from my clients when I ask them about how they think their problem or issue originated is, 'I don't know.' In response I always say, 'Whenever someone says, "I don't know," what I hear is, "I'd rather not know."'

The reason why people live in the 'I Don't Know Zone', as I call it, is because it's easier not to know. The challenge with these situations is that no matter how you ignore them, they won't go away and just get bigger as time goes by. Knowing usually brings a solution that results in change and it's easier to live in denial than face the truth. But if you decide to take it onboard you'll evolve faster than you will believe possible and will never have to encounter the same level of anxiety around that particular issue again. It's worth pushing through the fear barrier!

Embracing courage

The truth of this principle is that if you want to make significant changes in your life and start living your truth then you will have to embrace courage as your middle name. When I was going through major challenges in my life I decided to become Sidra 'Courageous' Jafri. Having courage does not mean fear does not exist, it means embracing the fear and still taking action on the things that require your attention.

Fear is actually your friend; it tries to keep you safe and protect you from pain. Accepting that fear can be your friend and communicating with it will give you the inspiration to take action on all those things you have been procrastinating.

If there is something you have decided you cannot do because fear is holding you back, that is the thing you must attempt to conquer! Once you let go of who you think you are, only then can you become true to yourself. Recognize that when life is easy and comfortable, there is no striving, no attaining wisdom. By embracing courage you will go deeper and meet those aspects of you that you didn't know existed before. Courage allows you to not only gain strength and be powerful, but also be open and honest with yourself. It's the way to live wholeheartedly.

Daily Practice: Make courage your middle name

You won't believe how much stronger you will be as a result of having courage as your middle name.

Take your Awakening journal and start by writing down ten areas of your life that you are currently procrastinating or self-sabotaging.

Now close your eyes and focus on your breath to quiet your mind and place your hands on your solar plexus, located between the bottom of your rib cage and belly button.

Now say to yourself, 'Through my connection with my courageous self and by making courage my middle name, I am connected to the greatest wisdom that is present within me. I acknowledge all the fears that I have experienced until now – the fears that have been manifesting in different forms of procrastination and self-sabotage. I recognize them as my friends and invite them to join me on my Awakening journey. I integrate all those parts of me that are afraid to move forward with love, compassion and courage. Thank you.'

Revisit what you wrote down about your self-sabotage patterns in your Awakening journal and write down the actions you are going to take as a result of being courageous.

Go through this process whenever you feel your friend fear kicking in, repeating the statement, 'I am safe' consistently, as this will allow the integration of courage with ease and grace.'

Living courageously

Now that you have courage as your middle name I strongly suggest you place a tick next to the some of the scary things that you haven't dared to do so far. That is what living courageously is all about: making the unknown, known. I love Sir Richard Branson's slogan: 'Screw it, let's do it!' I have used it many times to propel me toward the things I feared and sometimes with miraculous results. At other times I made a complete fool of myself! But at least I learned how not to do something and gave up being scared of giving it a go.

There are lessons to be learned in everything we do.

Another part of being courageous is being honest with the people that are most important in your life. When we speak our truth we are able to simply be ourselves. The problem is this isn't as easy as it should be. After all we live in a society that doesn't promote authentic conversations. A standard response to, 'How are you?' is usually, 'Not too bad' or 'Fine'. Anything other than these stock phrases comes as a surprise to us as we don't expect anyone to answer us honestly. After the response 'Not too bad', I usually ask 'If you are not too bad then what are you?'

I invite you to have courageous conversations with people and express how you are you truly feeling. You can make a list of those people you haven't been honest with and not communicated the truth to because you were afraid they might reject you. Embrace courage and have that conversation!

Surrender to the 'unknown'

There will be times when no matter how hard you try you will feel as though something is stopping you from taking a particular path through life. And in those cases it might not be self-sabotage that is holding you back, but the Universe trying to pull you in another direction. You'll know when this happens because the resistance you experience will feel alien. Usually the fear of change, denial or self-sabotage feels familiar on some level because it resonates with your own truth, even if you don't like it. But occasionally you'll just know you were not meant to experience a particular situation at that particular time.

I have seen it many times in my own life where I have assumed that I was procrastinating or self-sabotaging but it later turned out that if I had gone down that particular path it would have led to unwanted consequences.

LISTEN TO THE UNIVERSE

Naomi, a student, was living at home while she attended college in order to save money. She was fed up with the way her parents (as she put it) 'ran her life', and she was desperate for adventure. She decided to drop out of college and go backpacking with the boyfriend she'd just met. Her parents were very concerned, so Naomi lied and told them she'd arranged a job as a tour guide and that she'd go back to college after the summer. She was all packed and ready to go when she suddenly became so ill that she couldn't leave her bed. There was no way she was getting on a plane. To her despair the boyfriend said he wouldn't wait for her. Then, a few days later, the police came to the door. It turned out that Naomi's boyfriend had been arrested, for attempted drug smuggling! Naomi realized then how powerful a hold he'd had over her due to her desire for a more exciting life, and that the Universe had been sending her warning messages all along.

Beneath our conscious intelligence is a deeper intelligence at work: the evolved intelligence of the Universe that is taking care of everything. Surrender to that intelligence.

Knowing your soul purpose

Knowing our soul purpose gives us clarity on why we experience particularly puzzling or difficult challenges and can guide us on how to own them. Many people come to my live events looking for their 'purpose' but often it is associated with their career and they think that if they are earning money from their purpose then they are living it. But I don't believe our job is our only purpose. Our grand plan on the earth plane is to lift the Veil of Amnesia (see page 30) and experience life as the Source while integrating the qualities of the Universe, which include compassion, love, forgiveness, empowerment and kindness; this is our soul purpose. The earth plane is the only place where we experience duality: day and night, up and down, fear and faith, disempowerment and empowerment. It is the only place where the Source can experience itself through contrast.

If your soul purpose is to experience forgiveness then the only way you can experience that lesson is when you have been wronged. Just like the only way you can experience love is when you have experienced the lack of it. We choose a main theme for our incarnation (our eternal timeline) and then pick up different experiences in our current timeline that are in alignment with that theme. For example, I picked the experiences of self-harm and depression because they led me to integrate a lesson of self-love and compassion. To illustrate how these spiritual lessons can help us, I'd like to share Jane's story.

FINDING SOUL PURPOSE

Jane was feeling lost after the death of her husband. She was left with three small children and felt lost and purposeless. After going through the exercise overleaf, she gave colour to the movie of her life and picked up on themes of abandonment and disempowerment.

She suddenly realized that she had given her power away all her life: first to parents who sent her to boarding school, which she hated, and then to her husband who was loving but stifled her creativity. By using the Daily Practice 'Find your spiritual purpose', given on page 136, and reversing 'abandonment' and 'disempowerment', she found her soul purpose was 'adoption' and 'empowerment'.

She decided to deal with abandonment by actively 'taking on' friendships and new possibilities; ideas she had shunned previously because of a lack of confidence. And to empower her she found herself in situations where she needed to make her own decisions and take responsibility for herself. As a result,

> she grew as a person and became conscious of her own strength. She now looks at her husband's death as an experience that partly led her toward the fulfilment of her soul purpose.

In this way, we can see how life has two aspects to it: one is worldly and the other is spiritual. Both serve a purpose and work in alignment with each other. Your worldly purpose drives you to fulfil your material goals. Your soul purpose leads the way to achieve your soul's intention for connection to the Source. Your spiritual purpose filters through your physical purpose: the parents you picked, the school you went to, the career you chose are all are in alignment with your spiritual purpose.

Life becomes harmonious when both your worldly and spiritual purposes are in balance.

Daily Practice: Find your spiritual purpose

Take your Awakening journal and write down the story of your life so far as though it was a movie. Choose yourself as the leading role. Then decide:

- What is the title of your movie?
- What genre is it? Rom-com, sci-fi, drama, action, thriller, horror?
- Who are the main characters?

Write down the general story of your life, picking out any main emotional challenges or issues you have experienced. Take time to think about whether you have any repeating patterns or familiar themes.

Now write down what you think the opposite of those experiences would be like. These contrary story lines are the lessons your soul really wants to experience on the earth plane; this is your soul purpose.

The bridge

If you were attracted to this book, there's a good chance you're interested in self-development and have been immersed in the subject for years. I bet you have filled up many notepads with ideas and inspiring information about how to improve your life and have collected screeds of information with the intention that one day it will come in handy. But rarely do these things get acted on in real life. That's because often we work on developing our shelves rather than ourselves!

The bridge between knowing and owning is applying what we have learned. No matter how many resources we have, if we don't use them we just won't get the results. It's not about possessing the right books, tapes, oils, crystals or chants. All of this can be incredibly useful, healing and heartwarming but it can also be the vehicle for the ego to create the mere illusion of change, rather than change itself.

At this point in your Awakening journey you will have acquired transformational knowledge and skills on an intellectual level. You may understand the principles you have encountered so far. But do you really know them in your heart? If you haven't yet had an emotional response to the Awakening then you're well on the way to placing this book back on your bookshelf without really living and experiencing the principles in action. Living the principles can be compared to knowing water is wet and being in the rain. If you haven't been using the Daily Practices or the Divine Magic Statements and you haven't activated the earlier principles, then perhaps it's time to stop reading and revisit them.

Each principle is built upon the previous one. Once you own the first principle of Ask Quality Questions, only then will you be able to utilize the power of questions to Work On You. By working on you, you will understand that Awareness Is The Key and now know what is creating your reality. Now the Knowing Versus Owning principle teaches us that it's not only what you know, but also what you apply that creates the major difference. Real transformation is in the application of what you live in your everyday life.

> *The more you apply what you know, the better your chance to live an Awakened life.*

The shift only happens as much as your human psyche can handle. Sometimes you might not even see the results straight away. It can be frustrating when you are doing all the things you ought to be but nothing changes in your external reality. This is because every time you experience the information, it hits at a different level of knowing. Then before you know it, you will have changed as a person without even realizing it.

I have personally experienced this phenomenon. When the Awakening found me I knew I had a calling to facilitate people to wake up and live the truth of who they are. I needed to acquire certain skills to get my message across and enrolled on a public speaking course, which was something that had always terrified me. For the entire seven days of my course I became increasingly frustrated because although we were constantly working on exercises to build confidence, I still felt as scared as I did at the start. Fear coursed through by veins every time I thought about speaking in public.

After a particular exercise, I put my hand up and addressed the course leader by saying, 'This doesn't work as my fear is still not gone.' The tutor looked at me and smiled. He said, 'Look around you. There are over 300 people in this room. You put your hand up and passionately expressed your concern publicly.' Only then did I realize I was holding a microphone and speaking in front of hundreds of people without fainting. I had been learning, even though it did not feel like it. The information was having an effect, just as it did on this boy in this story.

THE SPIRITUAL QUEST

There was once an old man who wanted to teach his grandson about the sacred texts. The boy wanted to please his beloved grandfather so he kept studying with the old man, even though he could barely understand a word of the ancient scriptures. But one day he exclaimed in frustration, 'What's the point of reading this old stuff? We've been studying it for weeks and I still don't understand it!'

'Before I answer,' said the old man, indicating a basket in a corner, 'Please go and fill that with water.'

The boy was very surprised but did what his grandfather asked. Inevitably, all the water had leaked through the holes in the basket by the time he got back to the house. All the grandfather said was, 'Go back to the river and get some more!'

Three more times the old man sent the boy back to the river. Now the boy had had enough. 'Just give me a bucket! Baskets are no good for carrying water.'

His grandfather said, 'Wait. Look at the basket.' To the boy's amazement he saw that the wooden strips had swollen to close all the holes. Now the basket was solid and could hold water. 'This is how it works with the sacred texts,' said the old man. 'They transform who you are, without you even realizing.'

Living your truth

Now that you know you need to take action instead of just thinking about it, what are you going to do? As an Awakened being no matter what you do as a job, it is vital that you align your soul purpose with what you are looking to achieve on the earth plane. For example, if your soul needs to experience kindness, then volunteering at a hospice or an animal refuge would fulfil that purpose and will have a positive impact on your daily life.

Dedicate some of your time to others who have experienced the same fears or obstacles as you have, and see how they have overcome them. Volunteers are always welcome in hospitals and you will meet some of the most courageous, inspirational people there. Giving just a couple of hours a week for a cause that rings true with your purpose will bring you directly in touch with people and situations that you will resonate with and give you what you came here to experience. Whether you're concerned about children, environmental or political issues or food shortages, or want to help people who need your physical assistance, you'll find there's a charity or an organization looking for your support.

If you need to learn self-reliance it might be time to start up your own business. If trust is your issue look for experiences where you're in someone else's hands. This could mean quite literally as in being dependent on a partner when learning a martial art or relying on a partner in classical dance class. Or if there's something you've always wanted to do, a company you'd love to work for or someone you think could give you valuable information on a new career path – talk to them. Without the initial communication, nothing happens, so take courage as your middle name and make your move.

Sharing experiences can help inspire you to have the courage to try new things. Volunteering helps if your lesson is kindness or to learn to connect with other people's lives.

Daily Practice: Creating space

To see what really matters to you, you might find it helpful to simplify your life, as physical space creates mental space. An over-attachment to stuff can be draining, because all your time is spent thinking about your things. This creates a distraction and stops you connecting with your soul purpose.

Look at your possessions and ask yourself,

- Do I need it?
- Do I use it?
- Do I love it?

Keep it if you answered yes to any of these questions, otherwise give it to charity, recycle it or give it to someone who will value it. Get rid of anything that makes you feel guilty, sad, uncomfortable or anxious. When you clear space, new energy flows into your life.

Writing, painting, knitting or any other creative activity can also soothe your mind and give you space to think. Connecting with your creative side also helps you express subconscious feelings that need a voice. If you're not sure what direction to go in, making something will give you clues, and you don't even have to consciously think about it.

ACTIVATING THE FOURTH PRINCIPLE: KNOWING VERSUS OWNING

In the fourth step in the Awakening journey, Knowing Versus Owning, we've explored how fear and denial keep us in a place where we're Awakened in theory but not physically. Activating this principle therefore is about arming yourself with courage and diving deep into the painful emotions that are keeping you stuck. Each of the Awakening principles will increase your awareness, but to make changes you will need to make sure that you're doing the work too. From this place you can discover your soul purpose and align it with your earthly purpose, so that life begins to feel more balanced and true to you.

In the next principle, Energy Is Everything, we'll explore tuning into the invisible forces of the Universe and experiencing the heightened vibration that only comes from connecting to the Source.

Divine Magic Statement

I am the living embodiment of my truth. I walk my talk at all times.

Energy Is Everything

'We are all part of the one consciousness of love. When we are able to understand that everyone is composed of this same divine element, we will be able to open the door to this God-force energy in every aspect of our lives.'

James Van Praagh

If you look for something and you can't find it, does that mean it doesn't exist? Of course it doesn't, you are just not aware of where it is yet. The same idea applies to the fifth principle, Energy Is Everything, and accepting that just because you can't see your thoughts or emotions or God or the Universe with your physical eyes, doesn't mean they are not there. As Carl Sagan, an eminent US astronomer, astrophysicist and cosmologist said, 'The absence of evidence is not the evidence of absence.' When we learn to master energy by using the tools in the fifth principle, we raise our energetic vibration and our ability to connect with the divine Source of all creation.

Energetic beings

It's important to understand that I am not here to convince you that everything is energy and that we are all energetic beings; Albert Einstein proved that, decades ago. He demonstrated that what we see as solid is in fact waves of particles moving so slowly that they appear solid. He explained that everything is made of energy and therefore nothing ever vanishes, it just changes its energetic form. Moreover, everything in existence contains information. Thoughts, ideas and feelings are all energetic vibrations too, even though we can't see them in a physical sense. The thoughts you focus on the most create the reality you experience and so raising your energetic vibration also heightens your experience of life, both physically and spiritually.

However, since everything is energy and we are all energetic beings resonating at a certain frequency or vibration, then the Source or God or the Universe, however you prefer to think about it, which is behind all these things must be energy too – both with and without form. It is the creative force present in everything. Not only in people, animals, plants and 'living' things but also in our cars, workplace, homes, clothes, my pen and this book.

In spiritual texts, the world itself is said to be the thought of God or the divine Creator or Source but before anything turns into matter there is thought: formless thought. Wonderful inventions like the wheel, or aeroplanes or the Internet started out as a thought, as did darker creations like gunpowder or the atomic bomb. As the intention behind the thought takes shape the energy becomes focused on manifesting the thought's intention as a solid form.

If you trace it all back, everything comes from the same point of creation, the same Source, even though on the surface things might look completely different.

This realization alone rocked my foundations. I had grown up in a religious household where God 'above' dictated what I wore, ate, studied and how I behaved. God's rules were written in The Book and we had to follow everything to the letter. If we managed to please God, he had the power to send us to heaven.

I had imagined God, as many do, as a wonderful old man up in heaven with a long silver beard and a white robe. Most religions refer to God as a masculine figure; I think this is because on the earth plane men are associated with strength and power and God is 'all-powerful'. But many people who channel Source energy identify with a whole group of non-physical entities such as Abraham, Bashar or Orin rather than just one ultimate being. At one spiritual workshop I attended the facilitator used an acronym for God as: Group Of Deities: a deity being a divine or supernatural being. I choose to believe that the word 'deity' suggests a combination of different qualities of the divine. Therefore God or the Source is not just one energy but also all energy.

The Source is male and female, mother and father, nothing and everything. The Source is time, space, form and movement. At the same time, the Source is timeless, formless and motionless. We have to open our inner perception to make sense of it all because the real truth of the fifth principle is in recognizing and owning that the Source of all creation, which some people call God, is inside you.

Are you ready to meet the Source?

At my live Awakening events many people ask me the same question, 'Who is God?' Some of those people are angry with God for not listening, while others pray fervently according to their religious teachings and regularly attend a place of worship. I hear many stories of people praying hard to God, tears in their eyes, doing everything 'right' but they still suffer. Something in their lives still isn't working and it is causing them pain and sadness. In their darkest hour they pray, pray . . . then they stop. Slowly, they look around and find nothing. Then the horror of feeling abandoned by God, of God not listening to them, fills their being. Then they become angry and eventually reach the conclusion that God isn't there, He doesn't exist. This only creates more blockages in their life because in denouncing God, they are denying the God within themselves.

In my personal quest to find and meet God, I have flipped from one extreme to the other by religiously following every command to rejecting everything I knew about God. But I still found peace when I prayed. By praying I don't mean within the context of any particular religion. For me, praying means talking to that invisible Source inside you that you can't see physically but you know exists.

When I was at rock bottom and wanted it all to end I heard a voice in my head guiding me to educate myself. When I was struggling with my marriage I would talk to God constantly. I'd say, 'Take me' or 'Get me out of here'. I remember a random thought occurring to me at one of these low points, telling me to call a family member. That thought gave me the energy to get out of the house and talk to a friend. The more I listened, the clearer the 'thoughts' or the 'voice' became. Praying was giving me divine guidance.

I realized that what I call praying to an outside God was really connecting with the God inside myself. God doesn't go out and pray to anyone! God is God! God is experiencing itself through me! When I made that discovery I felt happy and sad at the same time. I was happy that there wasn't someone ignoring me. But I was sad too because if I was God, then why was I still in so much pain? Why was it that sometimes I got what I wanted and at other times nothing happened, no matter how hard I tried?

When I discovered the Veil of Amnesia, which I described earlier in the book (see page 30), it all clicked. When we separate ourselves from the Source when we are born our vibration is lowered, then when we reconnect it is restored to its divine state; and in-between is the Veil. It is the forgetfulness that keeps the experience on the earth plane exciting. We forget the truth of who we are and when we experience shame, guilt, anger and other energies that distort our vision, our vibration becomes dense and prevents us from seeing that the Source or God is part of us; it resides within.

If you are ready to meet God, then I suggest you look in the mirror.

The following story demonstrates how different our lives would be if we could not only see the Source in ourselves, but also in each other.

THE BUDDHA IN DISGUISE

After many years of fame a certain Buddhist monastery fell into disrepute. The chief monk was concerned by the decline in standards and the departure of many of the monks for other religious places. What's more, the monastery was not attracting any new novices. The chief monk travelled to a wise man and told him what had happened, insisting that he wanted with all his heart to restore the monastery to its former standing.

The sage told him, 'Your monastery is failing because the Buddha is living among you in disguise and you have not honoured Him.'

Confused, the monk hurried back. The Selfless One was at his monastery! Who could He be? Brother Norbu? No, he was lazy. Brother Pema? No, he was too stupid. But then the Buddha was in disguise. And what better disguise than laziness or stupidity?

He told the monks what the wise man had said. They, too, were taken aback and looked at each other with suspicion and awe. Which one of them was the Buddha? The disguise was perfect. Not knowing who

> he was, all the monks began to treat each other with the respect due to a Buddha. They once again practised meditation all day, and from all their faces an inner radiance shone that attracted many new novices and lay supporters. In no time at all the monastery was restored to its former position.

Sensing invisible energies

Invisible energies play a much bigger role in our lives than we give them credit. Have you ever thought of an old friend or relative whom you have not contacted for ages and they phone you? Or you bump into them? Have you ever been through a very tough time in your life, maybe financially, and a person who owes you money pays you back? These are all examples of when you have connected with, or transmitted, an invisible energy.

In 359 BCE the Greek physician Hippocrates said, 'There is a link, there is a bond, so to speak and even so-called inanimate objects have a form of communication.' In other words, the whole Universe is a living breathing entity and its various life forms, in all kingdoms, animals, plant, mineral and human, are not as removed from each other as previously thought.

Besides our five physical senses we also have access to the inner senses of our soul. Once we open ourselves to these invisible perceptions we can see, hear, smell, feel and even taste energies. These abilities are known as the 'clair' senses:

Clairvoyance
This is the most commonly known ability to sense invisible energies. If you are clairvoyant you can see events or images

that you cannot see through your usual sight. This information can also come through your dreams. When you learn to harness this 'clair', you will sense information that you wouldn't ordinarily be able to sense.

Clairaudience

This is when you perceive or hear sounds or words from sources beyond those of your normal hearing ability. You might hear names being called out, music or conversations.

Clairsentience

This is when you pick up information or sense energies somewhere in your body. Tingling or unexplained hot or cold spots are common effects of this sense. Psychometrics is a form of clairsentience used to describe when you can sense information about an object through your hands.

Clairalience

You experience clairalience when you smell energies, for example, perfume, smoke, food or flowers.

Clairgustance

This occurs when you taste a substance in your mouth when there's no ordinary reason for doing so.

Daily Practice: Which 'clair' are you?

You may already know which 'clair' you are but, if not, the following exercise can help you detect your dominant sense.

Describe your last vacation or your home by writing about it in some detail. Now have a closer look at the words you used to describe your story.

- If the majority of your piece contains visual details, such as colour and arrangement, your dominant 'clair' is clairvoyance.
- If you focused on sounds, you're in the clairaudient camp.
- If you mainly described the way you felt, physically, in relation to your story, you're probably clairsentient.
- If the smell of the place you described was particularly important, clairalience is probably your dominant sense.
- If you vividly described the taste of a meal you had, then you lean toward clairgustance.

Mastering your energy

Each of us is surrounded by an electromagnetic field known as an 'aura'. Your aura contains information about the physical, mental, emotional and spiritual energy that you are sending out into the world. The more conscious you become of your aura, the easier it will be to master your energy.

You may not realize it but you already have the ability to sense your aura's energies without even knowing it. For example, have you ever felt someone standing too close to you or sensed someone staring at you even though they were standing behind you? You were picking up on their presence in your auric energy field.

Daily Practice: Sensing your aura

I love using the power of energy to send love to the person in front of me. If you try this with someone you pass in the street it usually results in the person turning around and smiling at you. Ask a trusted friend to help you with this exercise and practise regularly until you have honed your skills.

Stand so that you are both facing each other. Take a couple of breaths in and out at the same time, while remaining still and quiet.

Each of you should now rub the palms of your hands together vigorously to build up a little friction. Then, at the same time as your friend, hold up your palms toward each other and slowly move them nearer your friend.

Soon you will be able to feel the presence of the energy field surrounding them. Their energy may vary, radiating outward more in some areas than in others.

After a short time, you will find that you can expand and contract your aura at will. When you want people to notice you, you can imagine your aura brightening and expanding. On the other hand, when you want to go unnoticed, you can retract your energy by imagining an invisibility cloak over your body. This is a very simple yet profound way of staying clear of unwarranted energies or attention.

Daily Practice: Surrender to divinity

Surrendering does not mean giving up. There is no urgency to manifest. You are allowing universal timing to help you manifest. Know that you will be happy when you get your dream and understand if you don't that it's because the Universe has something even better in store. Allow the Universe to take care of you.

Surrender your need to attach to the Universe with a little prayer, 'Higher levels please take charge and allow me to manifest my intention in this current reality if it is in my highest and for the good of all. If not, I am open to receiving something even better because I know I am supported, loved and taken care of.'

Breathe in the faith, knowing that you have set the law of attraction in motion and have aligned the soul plane with the earth plane.

Now you journey is compete, breathe in and out and become present in your body, happy that you have surrendered your outcome to the Universe.

Emotions are energy in motion

The feelings we label as anger, guilt, regret, shame, sadness, happiness, joy, love and peace are nothing more than energies resonating at different frequencies. Some of these energies resonate at a higher frequency and make us feel light and expansive. Other energies vibrate more slowly, making us feel dense and heavy and preventing our life force from flowing freely, which can manifest as illness or nagging ailments.

From a spiritual point of view, becoming ill could be viewed as an Awakening in itself, as it can be a pivotal period in your life that propels you in a new direction. For example, you may be forced to focus on dealing with the challenges that the illness brings. However, the Western scientific view of illness has brainwashed us into seeing disease as a random, meaningless event. If you get a headache, take a painkiller. If the gallbladder has issues, remove it. If you have anxiety or are going through depression then take medicine. We treat illness as a nuisance rather than treating it as a message we need to listen to. Symptoms are simply a sign that the body is malfunctioning and that you need to pay attention to it?

When we ignore what our body is trying to tell us we tend to pay with pain.

Science tells us that human beings are composed of our physical bodies, our minds, our emotions and the chemicals that fill in the spaces. All of these components affect each other to some degree, which means that there are many direct and indirect links between our mental and emotional state and our experience of physical pain.

To explain this more clearly, it might be helpful to think about your favourite person in the world: your partner, your child, a grandparent or best friend. How do they make you feel when you are around them? What symptoms or signs does your body give you to tell you that you love spending time with them? It might be happiness, joy or love. There is always an emotion tied to an experience. Just thinking of that person brings out all sorts of memories that you have stored in your subconscious, which produces an emotion related to that person. This is reflected in your body by how it responds to those memories and learning to read those signals can give you precious information about what is going on in your life.

UNDERSTANDING YOUR BODY'S MESSAGES
When I was pregnant with my first child, I was hospitalized for dehydration and kidney pains around six times, but it only ever happened during holidays and weekends. At the time, I didn't make any link with the recurring patterns of illness, but later it dawned on me that I manifested the illness for a very particular reason.

I lived with my then husband as part of a close-knit family, which meant that all of his siblings and their families would come and spend the weekends and holidays at our house. I didn't like this constant barrage of extended family since it meant that I didn't get the

> quality time I needed with my husband. There was no conscious way I could change this, so on a subconscious level I manifested illnesses in my body, which were severe enough to require me being hospitalized. This ensured that I got one-to-one attention from my husband, without the rest of the family being around.

I have also seen this phenomenon time and again in my clients' lives. For example, I had client with tinnitus in her right ear. After going through the ABC process (see page 37) with me she realized she created the condition because she didn't want to listen to men anymore. Another client was suffering from painful backache and was able to identify that the reason her back was hurting was due to taking responsibility for the whole family and felt that no one 'had her back'.

Everyone is unique, with their own symptoms that only they can truly know the meaning of, but if you want to learn more about identifying what certain symptoms may be telling you, then an excellent resource is Louise Hay's best-selling book *You Can Heal Your Life*. While working with clients, Louise noted how certain physical ailments were symptoms of emotional ailments and wrote down a detailed list of what each body area represented and its related dysfunction, and so was able to explain the connection between the mental pattern and the physical symptoms.

Money as energy

Thousands of people come to my live Awakening events and almost all of them are looking to make more money. Even though consciously they see money as the solution to all problems, they still don't understand the true essence of money. Let me ask you a question: What is money to you?

Whatever your response, let me tell you that your answer is a result of your conditioning and programming. Money is the core energy vibration of the earth plane and its energy is often misunderstood. Money is currently represented by plastic cards, paper bills and coins, which we use to buy things, but centuries ago it was pigs and chickens or bags of salt that were exchanged for goods or services. The definition of money has changed over time but even economists cannot agree on the actual meaning of money. From my point of view, money is how we exchange energy. The reason we have such big issues with money is usually a result of an energetic imprint, our programming, which we have learned or inherited from other people.

Money and wealth is not the same thing. Money is energy: you give or receive it in exchange for an experience. Wealth applies to all aspects of your life. Warren Buffet, the American business magnate and philanthropist, said, 'Wealth is what you have when all your money is taken away from you.' Wealth is abundance: how much of the good things you have in life.

Wealth is measured by the quality of your friendships, family, relationships, health and happiness.

If you think you are poor, it's because you are focusing on the money aspect of wealth. If you shake that feeling and replace it with thoughts like, 'I don't have stacks of money in the bank but I have amazing friends who will never see me go without', or concentrate on your lovely home, family or partner, then you'll realize that money is not to blame for your issues. When you focus on your wealth, your thoughts about money will be more positive so the energy will become more harmonious. Our experience of money can be separated into three areas:

1 Receiving

Look at your energy around receiving money. Do you think you are being paid enough? Are you finding it hard to find a job with good pay? If you think you are not being given enough money, then you have an energetic imbalance in your attitude to receiving money. Look at whether you think you really deserve to be given money. If you don't value yourself enough then you will be rejecting money on an energetic level. If you don't think you are worthy but want money to come to you, you have nothing of value to give in exchange.

2 Retaining

Do you hold on to your money or spend it? Lotto winners often go into meltdown when they find themselves unexpectedly rich because their attitude to money is the same as it was before. Look at your bank account and see where you owe money. If you give it all out to people you owe, then something in you really isn't comfortable with hanging on to it. Look back at a month when you had more money coming in than usual – how fast did you get rid of it again? As long as your focus is on spending money, you won't be rich! Many people have an invisible limit placed on how much money they can make because they don't feel comfortable making more. When you go over your limit you sabotage it.

3 Experiencing

Think of money as a way to buy an experience rather than spending it. Buying a car is experiencing a car, not spending money on it. Focus on the amazing thing you bought rather than feeling guilty about how much you spent. On the other hand, some people have loads of money in the bank but they can't bear the thought of parting with it because they're plagued with feelings of guilt, shame or other emotional blocks.

LOVE–HATE RELATIONSHIP

For as long as he could remember, 34-year-old Harvey had a love–hate relationship with money. An animated, intelligent guy, Harvey had gambled away every penny of his monthly pay, and not for the first time. He was a successful computer programmer who earned an above-average salary so he had plenty of money coming in but it was never enough.

When we talked about his attitude to money, he became very excited and spoke animatedly about the fortunes he had won and lost in casinos or the glamorous places he'd visited on the spur of the moment. However, he wanted better control over his finances so he could move out of the dingy apartment that he was sharing with someone he didn't even like.

I asked Harvey what money had meant to him when he was a child. He spoke very fondly about his dad saying that although he was bi-polar his father was a talented, self-employed boat designer. Harvey senior would swing from one extreme to the other, either working manically or not at all. Harvey's earlier years were peppered with incidents where the family home had to be sold to pay for Harvey's dad's debts, or where they would take a last-minute vacation in an exotic location. There was no middle ground, always boom or bust with extravagant purchases or fighting just to keep their heads above water.

Harvey loved his dad and didn't really question the situation as a child, but began to see that he had inherited his father's pattern. His cellular memory was calling him to repeat his dad's behaviour. As a result, he decided to change his relationship with money and to respect it so that it could give him excitement in other ways. He saw that he could use it more wisely to get his adrenalin rush.

He is now living in a lovely apartment near the sea and has taken up kite surfing.

There are four reasons why we sometimes don't make the money we truly deserve:

1 Fear of moving forward

One part of you wants to experience life as a rich person, but deep down there is a subconscious fear. Money is identity, it says, 'If I earn X amount of money I could live in a big house in an upmarket part of town.' Or, 'If I earn more money than my friends they will reject me.' You make judgments and fear being criticized. There is nothing more annoying than someone else being happy when you are not!

Ask yourself this question:

- Are you scared that if you make stacks of money you will move upscale and leave your friends and family behind because you won't share the same values any more?

You might be frightened of change, thinking your known hell is better than an unknown heaven. But change is the game of life and you need to embrace it to move forward. You may have subconscious thoughts that you're actually very comfortable with your pain around money. Maybe you're actually enjoying moaning about it because it is common ground you can share with your loved ones.

2 Values

You might want money but when it comes down to it your values might lie elsewhere. Look through your week and see where you spent most of your time. Don't include your job in this exercise because you're obliged to be there. Ask yourself:

- What did you spend your free time on out of choice?
- Did you spend most of it on money-generating activities or looking after your family or at the bar with your friends?

Maybe you value your time with your friends and family more than making money. Or bought into money myths – that going after money is greedy, there is not enough to go round or you have to work your fingers to the bone for money. Somebody, somewhere has told you there is not enough to go round and you believe that – that's why it's not showing up in your reality.

3 Beliefs

The reason why you're not making enough money is related to the beliefs you built up around having it. Ask yourself:

- If tomorrow you lost everything you owned how confident are you that you would get back on your feet?
- Do you feel life is a struggle and it's a pain to get money?
- Do you feel you can offer something worth paying for?
- Do you resent people who make more than you?
- Did you hear negative comments about money when you were growing up such as 'rich people are greedy' or 'you have to work hard to get your money'?
- Can you imagine yourself never ever worrying about money where you have unlimited funds to have anything you want?
- Do you believe that being rich will give you problems?
- How would your life shift if you had millions in the bank?
- Where would you live if you had millions in the bank?

4 Past programming

Your values around money were probably set by the time you were five when your caregivers, teachers and parent instilled their beliefs around money. If there's a little voice in your head saying, 'Please don't make money because only greedy people want lots of money and I'm not greedy', ask yourself:

- What were your parents' values when it came to money?
- Whose reality are you validating?

Daily Practice: Befriend, respect and appreciate money

To attract money and upgrade the energy of your financial situation, do these three things: befriend, respect and appreciate money. After all, why would money hang out with you if you curse it or get angry at it all the time?

Befriend it

Write a letter to your money and tell it that you've been playing hide and seek and you want to apologize.

Respect it

Money gives you the freedom to be, do and have what you want. If you don't respect it by giving it away or saying you don't care about it – you're only getting back the energy you have put into it. Respect where you spend it and stop abusing it. Or on the other hand, if you are a spendthrift and scared to part with it, use some of its energy to make you happier.

Appreciate it

Whenever you spend money, thank it for allowing you to purchase an experience. When you receive it, thank it for coming into your life. Love your money as an expression of energy – of love – it's you who has been abusing that love so give money a break! Don't deny yourself the love from money.

ACTIVATING THE FIFTH PRINCIPLE: ENERGY IS EVERYTHING

In the fifth step of the Awakening journey, Energy Is Everything, we start to sense how everything in the Universe is made up of invisible energetic vibrations, which while resonating at different frequencies emanate from the same Source. When we vibrate at a low frequency, we feel disconnected and weighed down with dense or stagnant energy. On the other hand, when we resonate at a higher vibration we are closer to our divinity and finding our purpose on both the soul and earth planes. Going through the experience of Awakening and learning to raise your vibration by activating this principle you will begin to see how the Universe has blessed you with the imagination to perceive what will make you feel most connected on a spiritual level. In turn, you'll experience the heightened energetic vibration that comes from living as one with the Source of all creation.

In the next principle, No Judgment, you'll discover your karmic and earthly connections and how to live more comfortably with the paradox that is judgment.

Divine Magic Statement

I am a divine expression of God. All of life comes to me with ease and grace.

No Judgment

'Be kind. For everyone you meet is fighting a battle.'
Plato

No Judgment, the sixth principle on the path to Awakening, is something of a paradox because it is impossible not to judge. You might find therefore that this principle proves to be the most challenging in your journey, it certainly was for me. The key to understanding how to activate this truth is to use discernment when judging and to let your opinions be flexible. This means to judge while being aware that you are judging. And when the judgment of an experience or another person is not serving you, be open to changing your opinion.

The irony of judgment

I freely admit that I spent much of my life judging myself and other people. Some I judged as being kind, caring and loving; others as mean, rude and selfish. I wasn't even aware that I was being judgmental until it cost me my relationships with my loved ones. I judged my circumstances – being born a girl, getting married young and moving to a different country – as being unfair or unhappy, which resulted in my depression, my self-harm and eventually my divorce.

The irony is that judgment is an essential step in our spiritual evolution. As a human soul experiencing this earth plane our understanding of judgment teaches us where our boundaries lie and how to remain in balance with the world around us. We must discover how to discriminate between good and bad, right and wrong, better and worse. Without these determinants, we would not experience the pain and desire to make things better for ourselves or anyone else.

Judging helps us to define a situation, problem or person: 'Is this going to affect me in a positive or negative way?', 'Is she right or wrong?', 'Should my children go to this school?' It is in effect your innate ability to make decisions and come to the best conclusion you can at that time. Without an opinion you wouldn't move forward or try to improve your circumstances, you'd accept them without thought. Very little would change in your life or anyone else's, and we would witness injustice or unfair treatment without reacting to it.

Judgment gives us the will to make a difference.

Our ability to judge shapes our individuality and powers our ego, which endeavours to protect us from being negatively judged. We enjoy expressing our opinion because it attracts other people with the same point of view and they, in turn, reinforce that we're 'right' about something. The more people agree with us, the greater our confidence and sense of empowerment. Sharing the same judgments with a large group of people can be a tremendous power for good or evil because we think that everyone who agrees with us is right, and that anyone who doesn't is either wrong or misguided. When enough people agree with us, we think our judgments must be true! Powerful convictions and shared beliefs lead to both great and terrible situations, from the Declaration of Human Rights to the Holocaust.

But without the things we have judged to be so dreadful, both on a global scale and of a personal nature, nothing good or enjoyable would exist. We would have nothing to compare it to! If everything was equally perfect, there would be no need for social justice, self-improvement or society, as we know it. Without the so-called bad guys, the game of life would not exist.

The judgment cycle

The trouble with judgment as a way of measuring ourselves is that it limits how much change can enter our life. When we form a judgment it creates a rigid and stagnant thought and doesn't allow life to flow or move forward. Even worse, once a person begins to judge their life, it forces them to push their own judgments outward and so they judge other people in order to maintain the balance of their judgment system.

If we force everyone to have all the same answers to life's challenges, we enter into a judgment zone where we might, for example, judge our partner for 'wasting time' and they judge us conversely for 'not having enough time'. Once a person makes a judgment, they very rarely take it back, which results in stress, pressure and conflict. The forcing of our values onto others is an attempt to maintain balance. But the only way to really create the equilibrium we desire is to relinquish our need to be the one who is in the 'right'.

You only really experience life from your own point of view, so remember that everyone else thinks they are right, too! It's a mind-boggling conundrum and one that disturbs our ego. We don't like feeling that we're less important than anyone else and on a primal, survival level, we cannot afford to. But if we ventured outside our overprotective ego shell and considered the world from other people's viewpoints, we might stop building such impenetrable walls around ourselves.

To experience our true nature we need to remain open to change, to be willing to lower the drawbridge and consider other values and opinions.

Do you want to be right
or do you want to be happy?

Instead of seeking power of others in our 'rightness' we can develop a better relationship with others by trying to see things from their perspective. This means we become more flexible and find change less painful. The best way to get off the judgmental rollercoaster is to form opinions that are fluid and can change according to the level of our awareness.

Personally, I found the sixth principle became easier to live once I had integrated Awareness Is The Key (the third principle) into my daily life. I realized it was my lack of awareness of the bigger picture that was keeping me stuck in the judgment cycle. The following story from the Taoist tradition demonstrates how keeping our opinions fluid helps deal with what the future may have in store.

THE FARMER

An old farmer was known throughout the district for his hard work. One day his horse escaped. His neighbours came over and told him they were sorry for his bad luck. 'Perhaps,' the farmer said.

The horse came back the next day, along with three wild horses. The neighbours congratulated the farmer on his good fortune. 'Perhaps,' he replied.

The following day, the farmer's son broke his leg when he tried to ride one of the new horses. The neighbours again came to commiserate with the farmer. 'Perhaps,' the old man said.

A week later a group of soldiers came to the village, looking for recruits for the army. They saw that the farmer's son had a broken leg and passed him as unfit for service. The neighbours congratulated the farmer on the young man's luck in escaping conscription. 'Perhaps,' commented the farmer.

The truth of your story

Your life is one grand story based on your values, judgments and memories. Believe it or not, at the core of any long-term suffering in your life is judgment because it decrees what you are going through is an absolute truth. But too often the truth you have come to believe is based on fading memories, other people's versions of what happened or your own manipulation of the memory to make it a better fit with your life's story.

If, for example, many of your judgments about people close to you come from your belief that you had a terrible childhood, what you decide to take from your current experiences will be coloured by your wish to reinforce that belief. That might be, for example, 'I am scared of having a close relationship because I didn't have a positive role model', or 'I overeat because we didn't have enough to eat when I was a child.' You may indeed have had experiences that formed those beliefs, but you're also more likely to forget or disregard the positive times because they don't support the story of who you are.

Even if the story you have built upon is based on 'real' events, as long as you cling to the 'truth' as an absolute measure of your life, you will miss out on the possibility of change and the variety that life has to offer.

Part of letting go of judgment's power over us is learning to release our memories that may not even be based in fact. All our experiences are subject to our opinions and judgments before we include them in the story of our life. We may even completely ignore something that happened that doesn't fit in with our current version of our story. And we may twist other things for emphasis or to strengthen our point of view or opinion. Our story is made up of elements of truth, fantasy and falseness, and we add colour or drama to make it less complicated or more interesting or to give us a feeling of control. That way, when things don't go our way, we can say, 'See, I was right! I knew that would never work out.'

The truth of how you view your life is based on your interpretation of the things that have happened to you. It is not the facts per se that are important but the meaning you give them. Once you understand that truth itself is not just facts, and that facts themselves are based on stories, you will learn to navigate your life with greater grace.

HOLDING ONTO RELATIONSHIPS

Terry and John were brothers. Both were intelligent men but they had major troubles when it came to holding onto relationships. In individual sessions, both brothers retrieved a similar event. When we dived deeper, we worked on one particular situation that was creating different issues for the brothers; they were both bullied at school when they were younger. Their mother went in to the school to complain to the head teacher, which resulted in both boys being called into to the principal's office to identify the bully.

Terry's memory echo from that time was that, 'Mother exposed my weakness. I trusted her with my

secret and was betrayed. Women can't be trusted' –
leading to his difficulty in relationships.

On the other hand, John's issue became obvious
when I looked at his echo from the same event, 'When
I get high grades, I get picked on and nobody wants to
be my friend.'

Terry and John experienced a completely different
reality, even though the event they experienced was
exactly the same. They both interpreted what had
happened in completely different ways. This happens
to all of us on a daily basis with every experience. Two
people watching the same movie will come out with a
completely different interpretation of what they just
watched. The challenge comes when you want to hold
on to your 'truth' or version of the events.

Part of releasing judgment is discovering how to embrace the
stories of your life, allowing different narratives to co-exist with
each other in harmony. Our belief that facts are unshakable truths
comes from the idea they are static. But facts become forgotten
or erroneous when new information changes or disproves them.

For centuries people believed that the world was flat until
new information caused an irreversible paradigm shift, a
revolution in the way they thought about and understood their
world. In the same way we used to think that the mind had
no connection to the body. But science has evolved and made
remarkable discoveries regarding the mind–body connection
and is beginning to recognize the powerful effects that our
thoughts and emotions have on our body.

The truth is that when facts evolve over time, they change
our inner model of the world too. Where previously, I would

judge people with a negative outlook on life, now I appreciate it is the meaning they have given to their stories that is creating their gloomy outlook on life.

When you hold the truth lightly and consider facts fleetingly it becomes possible to shift and change the meaning, opinion and judgments you make about your own life.

Reframing your story

Have you ever noticed how a picture looks different when you change the frame? The same is true of your story. When you learn to distinguish between fact and interpretation and change the meaning behind those facts then your entire story will change, if you want it to.

Daily Practice: Reframe your situation

Reframing is a very powerful tool from neuro-linguistic programming (NLP, see page 7) that can instantly transform your perspective to the possibility of a different interpretation. This process will also enable you to see the difference between the intentions and the behaviour of the people around you.

Pick a situation in your life that is holding you back. It could be not getting the job you want, a relationship that didn't work out or any challenging past experience.

Take your Awakening journal and write down the story of that event, and make sure you include a beginning, middle and end.

Now highlight the actual facts in the story and the points where you have interpreted those facts. For example, if you are working on a relationship you might say, 'He treated me badly because I am not bright enough.' The facts here might be that he treated you badly, but you interpreted the reason was that you are 'not bright enough'.

Now ask:

- What else could this mean?
- What if it means the exact opposite of what I thought?
- What if he treated me badly because he felt threatened by my intelligence?

Your reframe of this story could now be, 'He treated me badly because he felt threatened by my intelligence.' This liberates your harsh judgment of yourself, which could have been holding you back. Now use the ABC process (see page 37) to identify and release any trapped emotions around the memory.

Resolution after judgment

After I made peace with my judgmental behaviour and reframed the story of my divorce, my feeling toward the entire event changed. I even began to see that I had learned a great deal as a result of my marriage. Later, I was being interviewed on radio regarding my Awakening and I talked about how my ex-husband was a wonderful and supportive person. After the show I received messages from confused listeners saying, 'How can you be a good person if your husband was so nice and you still left him?'

When we accept opposing truths it can create confusion for other people. I accepted my husband as a wonderful man but I did not want to be his wife any more. Both sides are true and as an Awakened being it's important to recognize that we are all on the same side. Why, in a marriage separation, does one person have to be good and the other bad? Why can't two wonderful people have different values and make a decision to experience different lives?

Just as people judged my divorce, we are all conditioned to make snap judgments without thinking about whether there might be a bigger picture. Watch how you react to the following statements and answer the questions:

- Chris left his wife for another woman while she was pregnant. Is Chris selfish or a man in search of love?
- Penny works as a stripper in a nightclub. Is she cheap and soulless or someone who needs to pay for college?
- Alan owns five expensive cars. Is he indulging without thinking about people with greater needs than his or is he a man with a passion for automobiles?

How you judge yourself and others all comes down to your values. You will pass a judgment on the above statements based on what you value in life. If your core values are centred on family and responsibility then you will judge Chris to be irresponsible. On the other hand, if you value romantic love then you will judge him as in love or love struck. If you value education then you will admire Penny for her determination. If you value philanthropy then you will judge Alan as a self-indulgent guy.

Values

Your values are determined by where you choose to spend your time, money and energy. Values are the basis of all our relationships. When two people value the same thoughts, likes or opinions they connect and share a reality. You and I are connected through our shared values. I might not know your name, your face or where you come from, but I know you are on a journey with me to live an Awakened life. We share the same reality.

Conflict between people, organizations and governments is created by a lack of shared judgments. One party believes the other to be wrong because they do not share the same values. For the same reason, some people are extremely self-judgmental because their values are causing them conflict. Part of them values one thing but another part of them is experiencing difficulties with that value. For example:

- I want to have a close relationship *and* I like my own space.
- My work is vitally important *and* so is my family.
- I want to eat less *and* I don't want to waste food.
- I need to meditate *and* I need to exercise.
- I need more sleep *and* I want more time to be with my partner.
- Making money makes me happy *and* doing overtime is exhausting.

Daily Practice: Make peace with your true values

Identifying your conflicting values is the first step to resolving them. It is now time to work out which you need to prioritize. Once you have done that, make peace with the things that are not at the top of your list, it doesn't mean you don't think they deserve any of your energy, just that other parts of your life need it more.

Become fully present in your body by taking a few deep breaths.

Now, become aware of the first conflicting value you are currently experiencing in your life. Put both of your hands forward and ask the value to come toward your right hand. Acknowledge that part for coming forward.

Ask the other conflicting value to come forward to your left hand. Acknowledge that part too.

Say, 'I love you both. I am sorry that you are in conflict with each other. Please forgive me. I want to live a life of harmony and alignment. Please support me with my intention. I forgive you both for creating unintentional interference. With love, I let go of any vows, contracts, pacts and agreements that I made to either of you that stops us all from moving together with harmony. I declare it complete. We are all free. I release these energies from all levels, dimensions and timeframes. Higher levels please take charge and replace it with harmony. Thank you.'

Many people judge others and themselves for their behaviour without going deeper and finding out what they truly want for themselves. This manifests in judgment, criticism and jealousy, which are all dense energies that cloud our true natures and lower our energetic vibration. It's crucial to recognize that everything comes at a price. When you focus on one thing in life, other areas will become less important. You cannot devote the same amount of energy to everything, so you have to decide where your focus will lie.

MAKING PEACE

Alex wanted to run a successful business but had been struggling to get it up and running. For years, he judged himself as 'lazy', 'a procrastinator' and 'not good enough'. But when he looked at where he most enjoyed spending his time he saw clearly that he would much rather take his son to a soccer match than go out and make cold calls for his business. In the past, he judged himself for not being able to run a business but by using the Awakening process and resolving his conflicting beliefs he has made peace with himself. Now he realizes his son is more important and doesn't give himself a hard time about not working long hours to make money.

Awareness Is the key here: once you become aware of this truth, the activation of No Judgment will become much easier.

Judgments in society

In our consumer world, the acquisition of 'things' is judged to be the most important measure of progress or success. Judgments on what we ought to buy and the way we must look and behave are continually projected on to us by the media. As a result, it's not surprising that so many of us believe that to be beautiful we should have a body like a model, be under the age of 40, have blindingly white teeth and accept invasive surgery as an easy fix for all that is wrong with our bodies. To be judged successful we should drive an expensive car, have perfectly behaved children, vacation in certain locations and choose furniture or homes that create envy in our friends and peers.

There is a cloud of mass judgment that hovers over society. We might not consciously follow the trends in society but they are there in the background influencing our choices in order to increase the profits of multi-national companies. The 'ideals' are manufactured to make us feel bad about ourselves so we continually spend more money on products and services that will make us feel more desirable. We're praying to a false god with fake ideals so we can all continue to make more money.

It's almost as if we're a little hypnotized into believing that these ideals and judgments are 'real', because they provide us with a framework to compare ourselves with others. It's very challenging to awaken from this consumer slumber because if we are not even aware of what is going on then we unconsciously share the same values as part of the mass consciousness. Then no matter how absurd, we feel we all must be right.

Your first step to free yourself from the constant categorization of consumer judgment is to become more conscious of the messages aimed at you. Before you respond to any other external transmission, check within to see if you share the values and judgments contained in the advertising, marketing and branding aimed at you. When you become more aware of who is profiting from your 'failure' to live up to certain ideals and judgments, you will see how futile it is to try to attain the impossible dream of manufactured perfection.

When it comes down to it, the big secret that nobody in the consumer world wants you to know is that 'stuff' isn't going to make you any happier and that you are beautiful, and always have been. This is simply because, as I described on page 8 and explored in more depth in the fifth principle of Awakening, Energy Is Everything, we are all part of the same jigsaw. Just like every jigsaw has different pieces of various shapes and sizes, the same goes for us: we are different pieces of that puzzle. The more we become comfortable in our own skin and accept ourselves for who we are, the less we will buy into the judgment of society.

Guilt

After we have taken action to make something better, we often experience a stubborn form of self-judgment: guilt. But emotions, like everything else, are simply energy and therefore no emotion is good or bad; it is our judgment that makes it so. Judging an event with an attitude of 'should/shouldn't', 'could/couldn't', or 'would/wouldn't' lowers our vibration because it creates a dense and heavy feeling within the body. Or it might show up as an emotional symptom of anxiety or as a panic attack. However, when used in a way that serves us, guilt can encourage empathy for others and urge us to take corrective action to make things better. But if we feel continually guilty, not only for our actions but also for our thoughts it's time to examine what's going on in a deeper level.

SELF-TALK

Kim felt she was overweight and so lacked confidence in herself because of the way she looked. She said she was sick and tired of going on weight-loss programs that only seemed to work on a short-term basis.

In our first session, I asked her to keep a note of her self-talk throughout the day regarding food. She was shocked at the level of judgment she had. She found herself saying, 'I shouldn't be eating this', 'I know I must eat healthily but I just love 'junk' food', 'this is really bad for me but I don't care.' She didn't see how much her judgment around food was interfering with her intention of reaching ideal weight. It was making her feel continually guilty.

In my personal experience, I have seen that guilt sometimes reaches beyond our current timeline and has its roots in our ancestral timeline, especially when a child is born as result of an unplanned pregnancy or out of wedlock. Society might be consciously evolved from the 'obsolete' concept of the institution of marriage and now even accepts civil partnerships but our genes have still not updated from the indoctrination of 'right' and 'wrong'. This deep unconscious guilt can show itself as self-judgment.

GIVE UP ON GUILT

Natalia was 36 years old and struggling in almost every aspect of her life. She lived on her own and couldn't work due to chronic fatigue syndrome and was on government support. When we addressed the issue of guilt, her body started shaking and she curled up into a fetal position. In a deep meditative trance, she accessed a memory, which caused her to start crying uncontrollably as she remembered being unwanted: 'My parents. They are talking about abortion. I want to die.' Then she sobbed until her tears dried out.

After the storm of emotions had passed, she recognized the source of her guilt. She felt guilty for being alive! She didn't feel she deserved to be alive at all, which is why her life has been one long struggle. We carried out a guided forgiveness process, shown opposite in the Daily Practice, 'Addressing guilt', to help her connect energetically with her parents. Three months later, at my next Awakening event, Natalia looked well and was at the beginning of a promising new relationship that felt good to her.

Guilt is one of the most powerful emotions and can cripple our journey through life. Forgiveness is the antidote to guilt. When we look at life from our limited human perspective, we experience being wronged and treated unfairly, which creates guilt in the first place.

Daily Practice: Addressing guilt

The only way to address guilt is to rise above the limitation of our human condition and set ourselves free by forgiving all those who have contributed toward those feelings.

Start by getting your Awakening journal and a pen.

Take a few deep breaths, relax your mind and become present in your body.

Next, write the names of all the people you feel guilt toward. These could be people whom you feel you have wronged or who have behaved badly toward you in some way. Take your time and write down as many people as you like.

Look at what you have written and take three deep breaths. Imagine all the emotions you associate with these people leaving your body and going into the paper.

Now say, 'I love you, I am sorry that I couldn't see your truth and you couldn't see mine. I forgive you for all that you have contributed toward my life. Please forgive me. May we all integrate the lesson in the soul plane. May we receive the truth of these incidents. We are all now free. Thank you.'

Rip the paper into pieces and recycle it to the Universe however you see fit.

Life without judgment

To conquer our wish to judge others we should understand that people's stories are theirs to explore. We need to work on appreciating the uniqueness and individuality of the people around us. When we begin to appreciate people and their uniqueness then judgment transcends and opinions are formed. Remember that opinions are fluid and it's only when we become attached to our opinions that they solidify themselves into judgments. One of the many facets of judgment is prejudice. If you form solid opinions on something without having any evidence, you are prejudging.

Prejudice occurs when you want to agree with an idea without thinking about whether it has any merit. We often do it out of habit because we have always been prejudiced against a certain group of people or a particular idea, and GR Stephenson illustrated this in 1967 with his 'Cultural Acquisition of a Specific Learned Response Among Rhesus Monkeys' experiment.

RHESUS MONKEYS

High up at the top of the cage, well beyond the reach of the monkeys, there is a bunch of ripe bananas. Underneath the bananas is a ladder. The monkeys immediately spot the bananas and one begins to climb the ladder. As he does, however, the experimenter sprays him with a stream of cold water. Then he proceeds to spray each of the other monkeys. The monkey on the ladder scrambles off. All five monkeys sit for a time on the floor; they are wet, cold and bewildered. Soon, though, the temptation of the bananas is too great and another monkey begins to climb the ladder. Again, the experimenter sprays the monkey with cold water and all the other monkeys as well. When a third monkey tries to climb the ladder, the other monkeys, wanting to avoid the cold spray, pull him off the ladder and beat him.

Now one of the monkeys is removed and a new monkey is introduced to the cage. Spotting the bananas, he naively begins to climb the ladder. The other monkeys pull him off and beat him. Here's where it gets interesting . . . the experimenter removes a second of the original monkeys from the cage and replaces him with a new monkey. Again, the new monkey begins to climb the ladder and, again, the other monkeys pull him off, including the monkey who had never been sprayed. By the end of the experiment, none of the original monkeys were left and yet, despite none of them ever experiencing the cold, wet spray, they had all learned never to try and go for the bananas. This is the power of prejudice.

To activate No Judgment as a principle we must use discernment and keep our opinions pliable. Instead of stating negative expressions in response to something divisive use expressions such as, 'That was an interesting experience', or 'It is what it is', as these are some of the ways that can help us to rise above judgment and keep neutral. Most of the time people don't say what they truly want to because of the fear of judgment and that is exactly what holds them back.

You don't have to agree with people in order to love them.

Once you understand how judgment prevents you from becoming Awakened you may ask yourself, 'But how do I live without judging?' The truth is you can't, however, a problem only occurs when you hold on to your opinion as though it were the only truth.

To make it even more challenging, we force opinions onto others. When opinions are not allowed to shift over time, they slowly solidify into judgment. It becomes very difficult to change a judgment as the person making it has invested their beliefs and ideas into what has become a dense, immovable perception; the energy becomes stagnant. We don't want to change our judgments because it has taken time, energy and beliefs to create them.

Start to pay attention to your self-talk and the quality of your thoughts. When you catch a glimpse of yourself in the mirror, what do you hear being said back to you? When someone cuts you off in traffic, what dialogue takes place in your mind, or even aloud? What judgments do you make when a new person enters your social group? What are you observing about them and what opinions do their actions inspire in you?

Pay close attention and see how often you find yourself engaging in judgment. Notice how you interact when someone makes a comment regarding another person. Gossip is all about judgment! If you catch your mind making a judgment about someone else, let it go. Accept that you thought it, but remind yourself that when you judge someone else, it is a reflection on how you feel about yourself. Ask yourself these quality questions:

- What would you do if you thought nobody would judge you?
- How would your life be different?
- If nobody cared if you wore make-up, had a tidy house, read the 'right' newspaper or went to an acclaimed university, what would you do instead?

You really appreciate and value some of those things, but inevitably there will be others that you'll be relieved to let go of.

Knowing what you would do differently gives you an idea of what it would be like to be free.

It's so fascinating to realize how age changes the way we judge things. In our twenties, we are worried about what everyone thinks of us, moving into our forties, we don't really care what others think of us, and by the time we reach our sixties, we realize nobody was thinking about us in the first place because they were too busy thinking about themselves! You may be holding yourself back from experiencing your truth because you are worried about what other people will think of you – or even how you judge yourself. It's liberating to keep in mind that most of the time other people are too busy worrying about themselves to give what you've been up to a second thought!

ACTIVATING THE SIXTH PRINCIPLE: NO JUDGMENT

The sixth step of the Awakening journey, No Judgment, teaches us that our judgments are based upon the perceptions we have about the world and other people; and therefore they are the sum of our beliefs, values and life experiences. But no one person is better than another. Start loving yourself more and know that everyone is on their own life journey and that they too are trying to make sense of it all by being the best they can, exactly as you are doing. When you release judgment from your life you will come across a truth that shows you life is a fluid, constantly changing experience. Release your need to stick rigidly to certain opinions and ideas, and watch as your life carries you forward to a lighter, happier place.

In the next principle, It Takes One To See One, we'll explore how to discover your masks and how to live in peace with your shadow.

Divine Magic Statement

I fully accept and approve of myself.

It Takes One To See One

'There are two ways to experience this life. One is to keep wearing our masks; the other is to keep removing them.'

Sidra Jafri

In the seventh principle, It Takes One To See One, we will discover the universal law of cause and effect in action within our timelines. Like Newton's law that states, 'For every action there is an equal and opposite reaction', so we begin to realize that every thought, word and deed sets off a wave of energy throughout the Universe, which in turn creates an effect, whether desirable or undesirable. In the soul plane this is also part of our karma. In other words, nothing happens by chance and the people you meet, share your life with or even just know about from the news are all part of your Awakening journey; they are here to help you lift the Veil of Amnesia (see page 30) and teach you what you need for your soul to evolve.

We reap what we sow

Each truth we activate in the Awakening provides a foundation for the next one. This truth has its roots in Energy Is Everything (the fifth principle) because we are energetic beings and only attract what we need into our frequency. So what is showing up in your life right now is merely a reflection of the energy you are emanating in your beliefs, values, emotions, thoughts and so on. This principle is also connected to No Judgment (the sixth principle) because it's the judgment that lowers our frequency.

When I share the truth of this principle at my live event it often receives resistance. We are not willing to admit that the reason we are experiencing challenges in our lives is due to our external reality reflecting our inner turmoil. This means that if we are encountering stubbornness, selfishness or rudeness, we are emanating those qualities from somewhere inside us. On the other hand, if we are experiencing love, kindness and care, that is a reflection of us too. If the energy were not present within us, we wouldn't know what it looks or feels like.

Consider the following example: you are reading this book because you understand the language in which it is written. If it were written in a language foreign to you, first you would not pick it up and even if you did you would be unable to understand what it was all about. The words would not make any sense and therefore you would not be able to give any meaning to them. But because you understand the language, you are able to form a coherent meaning and connect to it. In the same way, each quality that you identify in another person is a quality that you are carrying within yourself. Each person is imprinted with the entire spectrum of all human characteristics.

Our judgment masks the traits we're uncomfortable with, preventing us from recognizing them as they truly are.

During my Awakening, I identified myself as a caring, generous and loving person, and simply could not see how I could be selfish, stubborn or rude. When I went through my divorce I magically embodied all the traits I had been denying. Previously, the very thought of being greedy, angry, hostile or manipulative was unacceptable to my subconscious mind, therefore it was hiding them deep within my psyche. I felt resentful and hurt at the outside world for being 'mean' to me, not knowing that it was 'me' that the world was mirroring back. It wasn't a 'bad' me, but, as Carl Jung, the famous Swiss psychologist described it, 'my shadow self'.

Masks of the shadow

Our shadow describes aspects of our personality that we are not consciously aware of. We then attract these aspects to us in the form of other people, events and emotions. Our shadow wears various masks so that we can maintain the image we wish to present to society. For example, if you find yourself talking about someone you don't like by saying, 'I am not like that', or 'I would never say that', or 'I don't have a shadow'. Then it's time to look at the mask you might be wearing.

> *Your shadow is everything you think you are not. It is everything you reject and hate in yourself because you think it is 'bad.'*

Unfortunately, all of those rejected aspects of yourself still remain within you and are covered up by your socially acceptable 'good' masks. The ultimate intention of being on the Awakening journey for all of us is to reconnect with Source – to become reunited with our true self and everything else in the Universe too.

The only way we can do that is by raising our energetic vibration. To fulfil that intention, we must first integrate all of our shadow by recognizing our masks and releasing the judgments we are holding on to. We can't see our own shadow, so the Universe sends us people or situations to serve as a mirror, which gives us an opportunity to see what requires attention within us. The following story demonstrates the seventh principle, It Takes One To See One, in action and illustrates how integrating our shadow helps us to embrace our true self.

THE STRUGGLE

A wise old Cherokee was experiencing a terrible internal struggle, and wanted to tell his grandson about it, to teach him about life. 'It is a fight,' he said, 'between two wolves. There's an evil wolf, who stands for rage, jealousy, sadness, regret, greed, arrogance, self-pity, guilt, bitterness, inferiority, deceit, false pride, superiority and selfishness. Then there's the good wolf, who stands for peace, love, joy, hope, serenity, humility, kindness, generosity, compassion, faith and truth. And this very same fight is taking place inside everyone in the world, including you.'

'Who will win?' asked the little boy. 'The evil wolf or the good wolf?'

His wise grandfather said, 'They both win if I feed them properly. If I only feed the good wolf, the bad wolf gets hungrier and hungrier, and never stops fighting the good wolf. He's always there, waiting for me to slip up, and when I do he pounces. But if I take notice of both wolves, then the evil wolf is happy and the good wolf is happy, too.

'The good wolf gives me empathy, love and an understanding of what is of the highest good. But I also need the traits of the evil wolf: determination, bravery, a powerful will and the ability to think strategically. The good wolf cannot give me these. I need both the wolves to keep each other in check. Feeding only one means starving the other, and one wolf alone would be too powerful for me to control.

'If you nurture both your wolves, they will serve you well and everything they do will be part of the great scheme of life. If you nourish both your wolves, neither wolf will feel it has to fight for your attention. And if the struggle within you of good versus evil is hushed, then you will be able to listen to the voice of inner knowing and let the higher good guide you in choosing the right path. Our Cherokee mission is peace. Inner peace means everything in life. Any man or woman, however wealthy, who is torn apart by inner struggle has nothing in this life.'

In the sixth principle, No Judgment, we established that judgment defines an experience in a certain way and stagnates your life flow. This means that your judgment of others doesn't really define them, it defines you. It doesn't stop the life flow in others, it prevents your own river of life from running.

When you acknowledge the information your shadow is displaying and accept its teachings, it dissipates.

Daily Practice: Uncover your masks

The following process will help you uncover your own masks that are mirrored back to you in other people and will help give you a choice to build real relationships based on truth in which you are simply your Awakened self.

Start by getting a pen and your Awakening journal and then make a list of qualities that you don't like in other people. Be honest.

Become fully present in your body and take a few deep breaths to bring your mind fully into the present.

Now, ask your body, 'If these qualities could live in my body, where would I sense them?'

Take all your attention and awareness into that part of your body and connect with the energy of the disliked quality.

In your mind's eye, allow the energy to leave your body and stand in front of you. If the quality you don't like reminds you of a person, then imagine them standing facing you. Or if the energy is not connected with anyone in particular, just imagine the energy to have a shape and colour of its own.

Now, address the person/energy by saying, 'I love you. I am sorry. Please forgive me for judging you and keeping you stuck. I forgive you for bringing out my shadow. We are both free. It is safe for us to remove our masks and allow the truth to shine through. Please remove and clear all traumatic experiences regarding this quality and replace it with love. Thank you.'

Repeat the process with each quality on your list.

Every event we experience is recorded in our body and subconscious mind. The shadow holds all the darkness from every traumatic event we have ever experienced and not cleared from our psyche. This is why our relationships are often entangled and complicated. Pema Chödrön, a notable ordained Buddhist nun and author, perfectly described this situation:

> 'Nothing ever goes away until it has taught us what we need to know. If we run a hundred miles an hour to the other end of the continent in order to get away from the obstacle, we find the very same problem waiting for us when we arrive.'

Experiencing the darkness

Everyone on the Awakening journey will go through this phase at some point, which is commonly known as 'the dark night of the soul'. This is the process where you realize that your ego is separate from your true self. It is when what used to make you happy doesn't do it for you any more because you were operating from your false self, not aligned to your true self, which is love.

When your ego senses that you are separating from it, it tightens its grip on you because it is fearful of the changes that lie ahead. Even though in reality this is a beautiful spiritual process, it can be a very difficult time; a crisis period in your life. Your soul is ready to raise its energetic frequency, bringing you nearer to the Source, but for this to happen you must let go of some of your earthly concerns. You may have to face your shadow in unexpected ways or find yourself in situations where you don't know how to continue. It's a testing time.

To see the beauty of your true nature, you must also embrace your dark truths.

At this time your life may feel uncomfortable or out of control but ultimately this is a healing crisis. Unfortunately, the human experience does not always feel good and our uncomfortable feelings are there to point us in a particular direction. If we continue to avoid these unpleasant feelings they will continue to influence our behaviour and will act like little magnets that continue to attract people and situations that we would rather not be involved with into our life.

Once all of the disowned aspects of our being are integrated we will no longer need to draw unpleasant situations into our lives. We will no longer attract relationships that show us the hidden aspects that we have been in denial about. We will no longer need another person to mirror our shadow back to us. We will naturally move toward those relationships that reflect back our light.

Living through the dark night

The best way to manage your 'dark night' is to surrender to it since the more you struggle to regain control of your ego, the more challenging things will get. The following Taoist story will give you an idea of how to be during the dark night of the soul.

GOING WITH THE FLOW

People watching from the bank were terrified when a man fell into a river flowing rapidly toward a huge waterfall. They could not believe it when he reappeared, unharmed, below the falls. 'How on earth did you survive that?' they asked. He replied: 'I survived by becoming like the water. I did not expect the water to be like me. I didn't think but simply let myself be moulded by the water. I fell into the swirling rapids and I came out with the swirling rapids.'

In the same way, this crisis in your Awakening is a natural one and it cannot harm you, even though you feel it might. The secret is to let it happen. Don't struggle, just go with it, honour the pain, acknowledge its presence and accept that it is part of a healing process. The Universe knows what it is doing with you. Surrender to love and trust that you are in safe hands. Just as day follows night, you will see the light again.

Daily Practice: Getting through the dark night

Using this simple process regularly can help raise your vibration during this difficult phase of your Awakening and help you to appreciate that, like everything, this too will pass.

Find a peaceful space where you won't be disturbed and relax there for a few minutes, focusing on your breath.

Then say, 'I ask light to be with me in my time of darkness and give me faith that I will see light again. Help me trust that I will come through this tunnel.'

Now, ask the light to show you the purpose of your dark time. Do you see any images or feel any emotions that give you clues to why you're going through this challenging time? If yes, write them down.

Imagine a ribbon of light, and see the ribbon come toward you. Take the end of the ribbon in your hand and tie it around your middle. Feel the love and strength from your bond. If you were given images or feelings to explore, do so now, have a think about what you were shown. If you don't have anything to work from, that's fine. You can ask again any time you like.

Mirror, mirror!

My divorce was the biggest catalyst for me to integrate my shadow. Initially, after the separation, I was living without my kids and I faced a lot of judgments around being 'a bad mother'. Every time I heard any comment on my motherhood, I would break down. One day when I was crying, my friend said, 'If what you say is true and the world only reflects back what we give out, then is there a part of you that believes you are a bad mother and people are just being mirrors to reflect that belief?'

This question opened up a completely new facet of the seventh principle, It Takes One To See One. Not only do people reflect our shadows, they also reflect our beliefs about ourselves. I went inside and explored the belief that I was a bad mother and, surprisingly, it felt true. After that, something magical started to happen. People started complementing me on being a 'role model' for my kids as I was teaching them how to follow their own heart. They could see that I was living a life that I believed in and I knew I was teaching them that being true to themselves was paramount.

Are there some people who still think I am a bad mother? Of course! But the difference is that I am neutral about their judgment and recognize that just like everyone is holding up a mirror for me, I am co-creating this experience and might be triggering their own shadows.

> *It's imperative to distinguish whose shadow it is and what requires attention because otherwise we are in danger of responding to people's beliefs without even knowing.*

KARMIC SHADOWS

When Padma moved jobs her heart sank when she discovered that a real troublemaker from her old job had also been hired at the new company she was joining. The two women had clashed when they had worked together years before when Padma was in a senior position to the other girl. But now she was Padma's boss.

She told me, 'She questioned my work constantly and made me feel that nothing I did was good enough. I felt so stressed out by the whole thing that I couldn't sleep properly. It felt way out of proportion and to make it worse my friends at work got on with her really well!'

I asked Padma what it was specifically that was so difficult about the colleague and Padma came to the conclusion that she was poking her where it hurt her most – because she herself felt that her skills weren't as impressive as she would have liked. Padma took this on board and worked on clearing her own feelings of self-doubt. Within a week the annoying colleague quit and Padma was offered her job!

This might sound like a coincidence but I have personally witnessed numerous cases like Padma's where a person received instant healing and an external shift when they went inside and worked on clearing their internal issues. I like to call this phenomenon 'unfinished business', which I classify as any lesson that you haven't integrated on a soul level from this lifetime or another.

Imagine each of your soul's lessons has a wire and an on/off switch attached to your body. Once you have integrated the lesson and are at peace with the issue there would be no connection and the switch would remain off. But while you still have unresolved energy present the switch is turned on to alert you. As a multi-faceted, multi-dimensional being you might not be consciously aware of these wires that are rooted in your current, eternal or even ancestral timelines, but the Universe uses every incident and circumstance you encounter to help you remember the points where these challenges were originally created so that you can become whole.

Karmic relationships and shadows

To help us integrate our shadows, I believe that we make contracts with different souls in the soul plane to teach specific lessons on the earth plane (see page 29). Once we integrate those lessons, one of two things will happen. Either that person will fizzle out from our reality and we won't need to deal with them again or the dynamics of the relationship will change. These are known as 'karmic relationships'.

LEARNING LESSONS IN A
KARMIC RELATIONSHIP

My client Lucy was softly spoken and had never learned to speak up for herself. Her childhood was challenging as her parents were domineering and often ignored or belittled her feelings while she was growing up.

For years she had been in a relationship with Simon, who was confident and outspoken, quite the opposite of her. Lucy's family did not approve of Simon, so they decided to elope, which led to her father disowning her. Months after they married, Simon's behaviour changed. He had tantrums where he would shove her and break anything he could get his hands on. He became verbally abusive and threatened to divorce her numerous times. Within a few months their relationship hit rock bottom and they were no longer sharing the same bed. Despite this, Simon financially supported Lucy's career and her expensive lifestyle.

Lucy cried during our session saying, 'I will divorce him and walk out as soon as I can find the strength.' I told her to look deeper, to think about what Simon could be mirroring or teaching her. I tried to make her see that, despite his behaviour, he was still on her side. She resisted the idea of a karmic relationship and said, 'All he's teaching me is how cruel men can be. Since I can't go back home, I'll find a new place to live.' With that, she ended the conversation and left.

A few months later I received a call from Lucy, she was very excited and said, 'You were right! Everything Simon did or didn't do was actually helping to teach me a lesson. No matter how ugly I got, he still loved me. I learned to scream, to shout and say everything I kept in my heart to him, instead of keeping it bottled up. Simon was reflecting my fears about sticking up for myself, which meant I was forced to be honest about my real feelings. All this bile and anger that came out of me had been trapped inside since I was a little girl and Simon's behaviour meant I could finally let the poison out. I don't even think he even really knew why he was acting as he did. But it had to happen otherwise the bitterness would have killed me.

Once Lucy recognized her shadow and integrated it, she was able to learn the soul lesson that she was being taught by Simon's behaviour and then they were able to enjoy the love they initially shared.

The law of karma states that, 'Every action has a reaction or a consequence', which means whatever you once caused you will experience the effect of the same energy. For example, if you have acted selfishly then you will be affected by others' selfish deeds so you learn to experience the effect your actions have on others.

High-frequency karma is generated by kindness and love in thoughts, words and actions. Using low-frequency thoughts, words and actions creates what is called 'karmic shadows'. The power of clearing karmic shadows blows me away every time I facilitate a clearing. What I have noticed, however, is that a karmic shadow doesn't have to be another person. You can create a karmic shadow with specific energies such as money, health or even around your relationships in general, rather than with particular individuals.

OVERCOMING KARMIC SHADOWS

Sandy had struggled financially all his life. He was a skilled salesman and had the potential of earning a lot of money but no matter what he did he couldn't hold down a job. We accessed his timelines with the intention of finding the point of creation of his challenge with money. In his eternal timeline, he saw himself as a very rich man who didn't appreciate how lucky he was and used his money to control other people. We carried out a process on completing his karma with money. He hit his sales target for the first time in years!

Another client, who had suffered a series of physical illnesses and debilitating health issues, received a similar result. Going through the ABC process (see page 37), she experienced an event when she had self-harmed and abused her body in her past lives. This had created a karmic shadow as she had carried this negative attitude toward her body into this lifetime. Once she declared her karma with her body complete and started respecting her body, her health improved significantly.

Daily Practice: Completing karma

Light a candle or incense to set the intention that you wish to integrate your karmic shadow regarding a specific issue you are going through in your life right now.

Take few deep breaths and become present in your body. Relax deeply and imagine you are on a wonderful deserted beach. Use all your senses to make the scene come alive; see the ocean, hear the crashing waves, feel the texture of the sand, taste the salty air.

Now, follow a path that leads you down a winding staircase made of sandstone. Keep going down the steps, knowing that it is the path that will lead you to somewhere really special. As you go deeper and deeper you find yourself entering a magical cave that is leading you into the underground. As you emerge into the underground landscape, look for a meeting place somewhere you feel safe and comfortable.

Hold the intention of accessing your karmic shadow and say this three times, 'I take 100 percent responsibility for my actions and non-actions. I am willing to integrate my karmic shadow and declare my karma complete at all levels, dimensions and timeframes.'

As you say these words, let yourself become aware of the energy of your karmic shadow in your body's consciousness. Connect with that energy and allow it to leave your body and stand in front of you.

Now say, 'With love and blessings, I let go of any karmic shadow that I created unintentionally in any of my lifetimes that no longer serves me. I forgive you and am forgiven. We are both free. I declare my karma complete.'

I suggest you do this process for three consecutive days to ensure clearing is complete.

Soul families

Many people experience the uncanny feeling of 'just knowing' someone when they first meet them. You've never had a conversation with that particular person or seen them before but something tells you that you have either known them from somewhere else or that you know they will be in your future. When you don't even know what someone's personality is like, or even whether you like that person or not yet, but you have a strong feeling of connection to them and they usually have a soul connection with you.

Your soul family consists of people you feel a bond with or a shared empathy and are often souls from many lifetimes ago who have agreed to play a supporting role in your life – or you have done so for them. They can show up in the form of friends, lovers, siblings, parents, teachers or even complete strangers. These are the people who 'get' you. Even though your soul family can be the same as your biological family sometimes, in my experience, soul family and biological family members are often not one and the same. Each serves a different purpose and contributes to a different lesson on your journey. These lessons might not necessarily involve being your friend.

The lessons we learn from our parents are often our most painful and emotional teachings. Your energy may feel heavy or dense around one or both of your parents as you have much to learn from them.

The souls that decide to become your parents in this lifetime might have a karmic relationship with you and are here for the betterment of your soul.

Daily Practice: Soul support

This guided meditation will help you recognize some of your soul family group and invite them to support you on your journey of Awakening. This insight will make life's more challenging transitions go smoothly as you will have the energetic support from the seen and the unseen world. It may be useful to read through this process first and remember the steps to allow for an uninterrupted flow. If your imagination creates any extra imagery or variations during the meditation, just go with it, as this is your intuition choosing the symbolism that resonates with you.

Find a relaxing place, where you won't be disturbed, and close your eyes. Take a few deep, cleansing breaths and feel centred in your body. Feel your energy shift as your earthly concerns drift away.

Imagine a golden ball of light emanating from the middle of your body that slowly encompasses you completely – like a bubble of light wrapping you in a cocoon. Feel the love, peace and wisdom that is present in you at this given moment.

Now, imagine yourself seated in the front row of a small theatre with the lights dimmed. Look toward the floodlit stage and ask for your soul support to appear. Now say, 'Friends of my soul, hear my call, together we stand to experience it all.'

Give some time for your request to be understood. Start to sense beings of light approaching the stage; these may show up in form of symbols or people you recognize from your past, present or future. The soul may be someone who has already passed over or someone you have yet to encounter because they are part of your future.

Acknowledge them by saying, 'Thank you for being a part of my soul family. I am willing to wake up to the truth of who I am. Please support me on this journey and help me to integrate the lessons that I signed up for.'

Imagine these beings transmitting light into your body and experience it entering your cells . . . This light is a connection between you and them. Imagine your

DNA being updated with this information as you receive
support from your soul family . . .

Now that you have made contact with those people that are
important to your spiritual evolution in this life, you will see
reassuring signs of their presence, which might turn up as
messages, images or symbols that will strike a chord with you
and nobody else. You can summon these people, or souls, at
any time by simply closing your eyes, relaxing and activating
your imagination, as described above. Your soul family can help
with all aspects of your life. All you have to do is acknowledge
them as a group and then speak to them about your problem,
aloud or in your mind. You can ask them to give you courage to
deal with questions that you find difficult to ask or to help you
understand challenging answers you have received.

While you are meditating you may hear a message, image
or symbol that provides you with a solution. Answers might
not happen when you are addressing them directly, but don't
let this concern you as your soul family always know the most
effective way for you to receive their wisdom. Sometimes,
hours after meditating with them, an inspiring thought will
occur to you when your conscious mind is relaxed and open.
Or you may see a clear message in a dream. This is a beautiful
sign that you have connected with your higher self through
your superconscious mind, which has then filtered through
your subconscious into your current reality. Pay close attention
to the answers offered as they are key to understanding more
about your soul purpose.

Group healing

Group healing is very powerful and can be helpful when you
are working through this principle as it can support you as

you integrate your shadow and masks. It is also in alignment with Work On You (the second principle). When people get together, for whatever reason, they have chosen to become part of the energy that is created by that group. Each group holds a specific set of intentions, beliefs and vibration. This group energy is often referred to as the 'vortex'. You'll know this is true if you have ever been to a concert or show, you become part of the concert that holds a certain intention. All the other spectators connect to you as you all become part of the same experience.

Whenever I deliver workshops either on- or offline, I always activate the vortex and ask all the participants to infuse their intentions within it. This allows all the participants to connect on an energetic level. From then onward, every conversation, process, discussion or piece of information aligns itself with the group energy.

By dealing with the issues of one person, we help the whole group. Consciously, the issue might not be relevant to the entire group but I have found that if the truth of that issue wasn't relevant to everyone in the group at some level, then it wouldn't have come up – purely because of the principle that you only receive what you give. Every time I facilitate a healing process, it affects the energy level of the entire group.

THE CIRCLE OF HEALING

On one particular occasion, I experienced the mysterious power of the vortex in a profound manner. I was facilitating what proved to be a particularly 'charged' healing event. There were about 70 of us sitting in a circle together, including a brother and sister. The brother decided to sit next to his sister, but surprisingly she screamed at him to move away, saying she hated him and didn't want to be anywhere near him. He was very upset and left the group. I tried to forget about the incident as we went through our different processes and meditations, but I had a growing sense of anger inside of me at this woman for humiliating her brother in front of everyone.

I decided not to speak to her about it that night, and after our next session we all went our separate ways. But later I was stewing in anger and also mystified – why did I care so much? What was in this for me? I felt a real connection with her brother, and that's when it dawned on me. I had desperately wanted such a brother when I was growing up. I was one of three girls and our mother lamented her lack of a boy all our lives. My sisters and I used to fantasize that a random boy would be delivered to our house, so that our family could be 'complete'. In my family, the arrival of a brother would have meant my mother would not have been so disappointed in me being a girl. A brother would have meant I would not have self-harmed or maybe even attempted suicide. And now for this girl to reject and humiliate her perfectly good brother . . . it was too much for me to take.

That night, I worked on integrating my shadow of jealously, resentment and anger around 'not having a brother'. This instantly calmed me and I started to feel neutral about the whole incident. The next day when we re-grouped, I expressed my gratitude for her allowing me to heal that part of me that I had repressed years ago and was creating subconscious interference in my relationships.

My live events, seminars and meetings quite often include people with similar energy patterns and issues. Many times people find their soul family in the group and have a feeling of coming home when they come to the event. People find friends who sometimes have been living parallel lives. For example, one woman sent me a wonderful message, thanking me for creating a safe space where she was able to tell the group about her mother committing suicide. She was shocked to find another woman whose mother had not only committed suicide, but who had also lived a very similar life to her when they were young. The two women became good friends and helped each other learn what they needed to learn, and so mutually deepened their Awakening.

Energetically speaking, there is no difference between you and another person. This is why you cannot hurt another without hurting yourself, nor help another without helping yourself. Divine love includes everything – it does not contain a single shred of judgment. So perhaps the most divine act we can perform is in loving every aspect of ourselves.

ACTIVATING THE SEVENTH PRINCIPLE: IT TAKES ONE TO SEE ONE

In the seventh step of the Awakening journey, It Takes One To See One, we find that while some people bring difficult choices and emotions into our lives there are those who bring love, joy, kindness and laughter. To activate this principle you'll need to think about those you love – who they are and why you care about them. Just as you have identified the negative things you don't like seeing mirrored back, it's just as important to understand the goodness in you that you see reflected in others. All that love and happiness is a true reflection of your own capacity to love. All the wonder, excitement, energy and curiosity that other people or situations bring to your surface is available to you, living and breathing inside of you already – waiting to be realized once again. All you need to do to connect with the love, hope and cheer in your life is to remember it, think of it and let its vibration take over.

In the next principle, Nothing Is Missing, we'll explore discovering the lessons you need to learn on the earth plane in order to discover your soul purpose.

Divine Magic Statement

I welcome all those parts of me that I have left behind in space, time and reality. I am whole.

THE EIGHTH PRINCIPLE

Nothing Is Missing

'Be content with what you have; rejoice in the way things are. When you realize there is nothing lacking, the whole world belongs to you.'

Lao Tzu

In the eighth principle of Awakening we'll observe how the Universe conspires to give us everything we need to fulfil our requirements to integrate our soul lesson on this earth – each sweetness of love, every bitterness of disappointment. Loss and hurt are all a part of a bigger plan for us to transform into who we are meant to be. Our experiences equip us with our own unique form of wisdom and particular set of gifts that we are here to offer to the world. Once we remove our ego's distorted version of reality and wear the glasses of our soul, we are able to see the hidden gifts in all the challenges, difficulties and circumstances that life presents to help us to grow, evolve and become a better person.

Embracing life

Nothing Is Missing is one of the simplest and yet the most complicated of principles. The reason why this truth shows up at the later stage of our Awakening journey is because it integrates with all the previous seven principles. How easy or difficult you find this truth is entirely based on how much you have absorbed from the ones that came before. If you haven't aligned yourself with the sixth principle, No Judgment, then your ego might experience challenges in accepting Nothing Is Missing. You might be thinking, 'All the suffering in the world: bullying, rape, murder, abuse! Surely this can't be perfect and there is something missing for all this pain to show up.'

BECOMING A LIFELINE

'How can you say that, do you even know what I have gone through?' This was the reaction I got from one woman when I explained the eighth principle, Nothing Is Missing, at an Awakening seminar. I took a deep breath, knowing that this truth usually hits people's core vibration of victim consciousness. I responded by asking her to share her journey.

She had lost five children, all of them before they turned 18: two in a car accident, one to meningitis and the other two to sudden infant death syndrome that ran in her family, unbeknown to them all. She had lost all faith in any higher power and felt unloved by the Universe. I felt her pain as she broke down while sharing her story.

Afterwards, I asked her to think about what she has achieved as a result of what happened to her – things she wouldn't have taken on if she hadn't lost her children. She told the group that she ran the largest bereavement centre in her area, where she helps parents heal after the loss of newborns or miscarriages. She feels fulfilled and rewarded when a mother leaves her care feeling a little lighter.

Later she told me how grateful she felt for the seminar because she hadn't really thought of the link between what had happened to her and how much her experiences contributed to her being such a lifeline for others in the same situation.

For years I struggled to understand why certain things had happened in my life. I had never thought that my parents would disown me for a time in my life, or that I would live for a while without my children. One day I was sitting with my spiritual teacher, who saw the pain in my eyes and asked me, 'Do you know why your parents don't talk to you or your kids don't live with you?' I shook my head and he said, 'Look closely at your life and tell me what you feel most passionate about.' I knew my answer instantly, the Awakening, not my parents, religion, teachers or environment.

He said, 'Exactly. That's why this is happening. The Universe loves you so much that it wants you to find out your own truth, which is why the divorce happened so that you could be disowned by your parents and ostracized by your community and find the real you. It is such a gift!' These words changed my whole point of view on my life's events and I felt like the man in the following story.

THE RESCUE

After his ship sank, a sailor was washed up on a desert island. The only crew member to survive the wreck, he called constantly upon God for help. Day after day he expected to see a ship coming to his rescue, but the sea remained empty. In despair he nevertheless managed to make a shelter out of some planks from the wreck that drifted onto the shore.

He was in the water one day trying to catch fish when he noticed clouds of smoke over the beach. He rushed back to the hut to find his worst fears confirmed: the hut was on fire and everything he had made for himself had been destroyed. 'Why me?' he cried, maddened by despair.

The man was stunned the next morning when he woke up and saw a ship approaching the island. 'How on earth did you find me?' he called out. Confused, the sailors replied, 'But we saw the big smoke signal you made yesterday!'

This is exactly what every event in our lives is about, should we choose to embrace this truth. It's easy to get discouraged when things aren't going according to how we planned it, as our egos like to control every situation and expect a certain outcome. From the soul's point of view, it's all working according to a divine plan, even your pain and suffering serve a great purpose on your journey of Awakening.

Greater purpose

My favourite acronym for SOUL is: School Of Unlimited Life, which was devised by Jennifer Hough, an inspirational writer and speaker and one of my great teachers who showed me my greater purpose in life. By integrating her teachings, I found my SOUL. I started seeing that each lifetime can be classified as a semester where we pick the 'subjects' in the form of lessons such as forgiveness, kindness, self-love and many more.

The lessons we choose are determined by the stage of our soul and the integration of that lesson. If you miss a lesson in a particular semester, then you can pick the same lesson in the next alongside other lessons. After all, it is the School of Unlimited Life, so it doesn't really matter how many semesters it takes you to integrate a lesson and move on to a more evolved lesson. The only difference that happens is that the longer it takes to complete a lesson, the thicker the Veil of Amnesia (see page 30) becomes. The more semesters it takes you to complete a lesson, the more dramatic the circumstances your soul might pick to make sure you burn through the Veil.

Therefore, the defining idea behind the eighth principle is recognizing our destiny, our soul purpose, so that we can embrace every experience and integrate our lessons with ease and grace.

Every experience then becomes an unfolding part of our destiny.

Who have you become?

I am sure that when you were growing up you faced the inevitable question, 'What do you want to be when you grow up?' My answer to that question kept changing according to which phase of life I was in. I went from wanting to be a doctor to a singer, from an entrepreneur to an artist. This resulted in two degrees, a few diplomas and attending unlimited workshops and courses. I was chasing a dream. A dream that I wasn't even sure was mine or not. I had no clue what I wanted. I used to think to myself, 'When I get there, everything will be fine.' But every time I used to 'get there', as if by magic, another 'there' would suddenly appear, and then another one.

When I was struggling with my studies, I used to think, 'When this is over, then everything will be better.' Then I got married and started struggling and thought, 'When I complete my degree, then I'll be happy.' Then I thought, 'When I start working. . .' Then, 'When I get a bigger house . . .' Then, 'When I drive a Mercedes . . .' Then, 'When I get a housekeeper. . .' And then? This kept happening until one day I had all of the things I had wanted and still something was missing! I realized that no matter how hard I tried, I was always chasing something. It's only when I stopped chasing the external reality of 'getting there' that I started noticing how each experience and challenge in my life was building me up to be the person that I am now.

I wrote down all my failures and missed opportunities and activated the first principle, Ask Quality Questions, and really thought about who I had become and what I had discovered because of my 'mistakes'. I started seeing the thread of perfection in every experience. For example, I failed an entrance test exam to a highly reputable school where I could have had an option to become a doctor. That failure led to my enrollment at a school that focused on commerce, which later helped me in my business degree. My failed marriage has lead me to become the best version of myself and has allowed me to serve thousands of people across the world, which I wouldn't have been able to do had I been living my 'dream married life'. In fact, you wouldn't be reading this book had I not gone through every single experience in my life.

Daily Practice: What your failures have taught you

Awaken to the idea that your failures are part of your success. Make a list of all of the failures that you have experienced. Next to each failure, write the answer to the following questions,

- What was the gift in this?

- What did I learn as a result of going through that?

Write down any emotions that come up as a result of reliving the memory of your perceived failure. Feelings of guilt, regret, shame or fear might resurface. Then use the ABC process (page 37) to heal the situation.

Stop the chase

Many clients, like the one described in the following story, come to me with the same challenge. They feel they are always chasing deadlines, clients, jobs, time, health and money. Society deems us to be successful when we have perfect bodies, lots of money and are living the life of our dreams with the people we love. Anything less than this is judged to be imperfect and creates a void in people.

QUIT WORRYING ABOUT THE 'SHOULDS'
Sophie had been experiencing depression for around three months when she came to see me for help. Upon inquiry, she said she felt like a failure because she thought she should play a bigger game in life. I asked her where she got the idea that she had failed from.

She was 60 years old and had run a local cafe for the last 35 years, her kids had grown up and she had a group of friends and family around her. She said she went to a business seminar a few months ago, where the speaker suggested that you can be, do and have anything you want but you must dream big. At the seminar she created a vision board around selling her cafe and house and travelling the world to fulfil her longing for adventure. But nothing really changed after the course and she kept on living the same life. This left her feeling really depressed.

I asked her to tell me about her ultimate dream after she had returned from travelling. She said, 'I want to buy a place where I can be near my friends and family and spend time with my grandchildren. I also want to teach people how to bake cakes at the local community centre. I asked her what she was doing right now and she said she was living near her friends and family, helped with her grandchildren, baked cakes and served the local community through her cafe.

At that point, of course, she became aware that she had bought into someone else's reality, which meant that she was sold an idea of a perfect life that wasn't actually hers, or even appropriate to where she was in her life.

There are many of us who buy into the idea of how our lives 'should' look; if they don't look like that we get sad and anxious. Nothing Is Missing teaches us to live in the present. It helps us to acknowledge that the future does not exist, as it has not yet arrived; and nobody really knows what it might bring. You only have the now.

An Awakened being knows that life can be found only in the present moment – these moments are what life is. You accept reality as it is, not as you think it is, wish it was or hope or fear it may be. The present moment connects with life itself. The best way you can appreciate your divinity, your role as part of the Source, is to live your life in the best way you know how. So the best way to appreciate the Universe is by letting go of all that happened in the past.

> *Whatever life has taken away from you, release it, you no longer need it.*

When you surrender and let go, you allow yourself to bask in your own divine glory in the moment. Letting go of the past means you can enjoy everything that is happening right now. When you are depressed it means you are living in the past. When you are anxious that means you are living in the future. The best space to be in is the present. Past, present and future are all in the matrix, happening right here, right now.

Daily Practice: Being present

This simple yet powerful process will help you bring all your energies from past or future into the present.

Find a peaceful space where you won't be disturbed and relax there for a few minutes, focusing on your breath. Allow yourself to relax deeply.

Imagine you are standing on a beach. The sun is shining, gently warming your skin, and you can feel the golden sand beneath your feet. Imagine a sparkling blue sea in front of you as you listen to the sound of the waves and smell the salt water in the air.

Look over your left shoulder – all that you see represents your past.

Look over your right shoulder, all that you see represents your future.

Look up, that represents the divine masculine expression of Source, the father and light.

Look down, that represents the divine feminine expression of Source, the mother and love.

After bringing all your attention to the present moment, right here, right now, say, 'Melt any memories that no longer serve me. May I dwell in the heart of the divine presence. May I know the deepest levels of peace. May I be held in the grace of the beloved. May I surrender completely into the joy of my own true nature of experiencing this dimension in the earth plane.'

Destiny and free will

The topic of destiny and free will is an interesting one. Some people believe in destiny to the degree that they refuse to take any actions as they believe, 'If it's meant to be, I can't stop it. If it's not meant to be, I can't make it happen.' Which sometimes works in their favour but at other times, when it doesn't, they call it 'fate'. Others live by the statement, 'If it's to be, it's up to me.' There is nothing outside of themselves they can rely on and they have to create their own paths. Both ways have their own ups and downs. The first belief releases a person from taking any responsibility and the second doesn't leave any room for miracles and support from the Universe.

My own version of destiny is that life consists of the challenges, lessons and life skills our soul chose to master before we incarnated in order to experience the School of Unlimited Life. Your free will gives you the choice to react to the challenges that are presented in this lifetime. There is a grand plan, which you have designed and you carefully chose people who were willing to teach you the lessons you need to learn on this earth plane.

The Veil of Amnesia (see page 30) that descends between lifetimes keeps your past lives invisible so that you can engage your free will. It's important to recognize at this point that your free will is usually based on your own programming in this lifetime. So we react to a situation mostly from our subconscious mind, which is why integrating the earlier Awakening principles is imperative to give you a choice in how to react. When your personality is not willing to align with the soul's purpose on a subconscious level and experiences disconnection from the Source, the reactions are often full of hurt, disappointment and anger. Your decision not to participate is always respected. If the soul purpose is not completed by the end of your lifetime then this information will be stored to continue in another lifetime.

Your lessons are kept in your Akashic Record (see page 13) and sometimes a major life-changing event is required to Awaken from lifetimes of rejecting a lesson. Terminal illness or losing a loved one can be a pivotal period that propels you to look for a new way of being. Like Betty in the following story, you might literally be forced to stop living your life the way it was and start to become aware of why things happened so that you can be given the chance to change your course of action.

WHY ME?

Betty was married for 20 years to a husband who didn't treat her very well. When she was younger her father abused her in a similar way to her husband. She was a mother of two teenage boys who didn't respect her and showed every sign of following in their dad's footsteps.

She was pregnant with their third child when she found out that she had cancer. She was devastated. She had suffered all her life and couldn't make sense of why these 'bad' things were happening in her life. As she wasn't aware of her soul's purpose, she had been exercising her free will not to accept the lesson. I asked her if she was open to the idea of past lives and that her soul was trying to integrate a major lesson through these events. I told her she didn't have to believe in it, just to be open and receptive to seeing her life from a different point of view.

She agreed and we started to activate the principles. She wrote the story of her life as though it were a movie (covered in the fourth principle, Knowing Versus Owning) to pick up her life's theme and purpose and found the answer was staring in her face! All her life Betty had been surrounded by abusive men: father, husband and sons. They were all teaching her the same lesson: 'self-love and self-respect'. As she failed to integrate the lesson and kept building up resentment toward men, she manifested cancer while pregnant with her third boy!

Then, because giving birth to her baby would probably kill her in her weakened state, Betty had to choose her own life over her unborn child's. She made the tough decision to abort her unborn baby so that she could have cancer treatment. We did a major healing session where she forgave all the men in her life and finally she was able to integrate her lesson of 'self-love'.

This resulted in a drastic change in her relationships, especially with her husband. When she first came to me, after finding out she had cancer, her husband registered on a dating website claiming he was 'widowed' and spoke to her about selling her jewellery and her assets. Later, he changed his attitude and started telling their boys to 'respect' their mother and supported her through chemotherapy.

Co-creating your destiny

I believe that when we live as an Awakened being we are able to discover our soul purpose and with free will we are able to co-create our destiny. One important factor that plays a major role in destiny is karma, and in the seventh principle, It Takes One To See One, I describe how to release yourself from karma that no longer serves you. In this principle, we will look at the other side of karma and how you can use karma to improve your life and fulfil your soul's purpose.

I was fortunate enough to grow up in a family where both of my parents were helpful, kind and generous people who served family and friends unconditionally. They would help strangers with food, clothes, money or physical labour. Giving came naturally to me as a result of observing their generosity. My mother always donated to charities whenever there was an exam or potential challenge in our lives. I later realized she was attempting to gain 'karmic brownie points' from the Universe.

As an Awakened being we know that the only way to deal with the Universe is to do good deeds without expecting a return from any individual. So whenever you help someone or give any kind of help, it has to be with the pure intention of helping the 'Source's creation' and not the person in front of you personally. I truly recognized the power of this phenomenon around the most challenging time of my life, my divorce.

After my separation, when I was struggling financially and praying to God to help me, I received a phone call out of the blue from a friend whom I had lost touch with for a few years. She said, 'I heard about your divorce, how are you?' I told her I was OK but a bit worried about finances. She said, 'Are you crazy, why didn't you tell me, I owe you money.' I couldn't believe it and she reminded me that three years ago, when she was buying a house, I lent her quite a large sum of money toward her deposit. I went into complete appreciation of how the Universe rewarded me in the most amazing way.

Similarly, I have experienced countless moments of unexpected financial support from friends who just showed up at the right time. I see these 'lucky' turns as a result of karmic brownie points I have invested into the Universe.

I often get asked about 'my secret' of success and how I went from being in debt to running an international business. My answer is simple! I deal with God (or the Source). I take care of God's creation and God takes care of me! I treat anyone who shows up in my reality as an expression of God and support them, not because of who they are in their physical bodies but whom they represent in their spirit bodies. The truth of how your karma influences your destiny is demonstrated wonderfully in the following story.

THE TWO NEIGHBOURS

Once upon a time there was a pious man who tried to be generous and just in his dealings with everyone. This good man had a neighbour who was lazy and a drunkard and would sit on his porch shouting insults at anyone who passed by. One day both men happened to take a trip into town. On the way back the pious man fell in the road and hurt his knee so badly that he could barely hobble home.

A little later the rude drunkard was returning to his house when he came across a bag filled with money at the very point where his neighbour had hurt himself! The pious man was upset and furious when he heard what had happened and went to consult the local sage. 'Why did God allow this?' he asked. 'I pray in the temple every day. I do my best to put others before myself. I try with all my heart to be a good person, every day. And yet this man is rewarded, not me!'

The sage answered, 'Do not presume to question the ways of the Lord. It was written in the stars that today you would die because of your actions in your past lives. Yet by your actions in this life you have overcome your karma and instead of death you have suffered only injury. Your neighbour's karma was to become the ruler of this land. Yet he, too, has overcome his karma, by choosing of his own free will to abuse his body and insult other people, to steal and to be cruel. Instead of a whole kingdom he has received a small bag of coins. So be grateful that God has given you the chance to escape the karma of your past lives, and instead permits you to create your own fate by acting through your free will.

Remember that most of the time we are influenced by the Veil of Amnesia (see page 30) and are not aware of the choices we have in reacting to any given challenge. Whenever I share the power of co-creating destiny, I get asked the question, 'If everything is a co-creation of destiny, then all the suffering, abuse, child labour, human trafficking, wars would be part of co-creation too. Can we blame those victims for having created all of the pain themselves?'

My response to that is, 'Of course! As human beings we haven't picked those challenges as a choice, but as a spiritual being we are powerful co-creators in human form and all it requires is rising above our limited human perspective of a situation and seeing it from the eyes of our souls. The question that can provide you insight into your own soul's destiny is:

What is it that my soul is looking to experience as a result of this crisis?

Daily Practice: Crisis creates opportunities for growth!

Have a long think about the biggest crisis you have had to face in your life, a time when something happened to you that you felt was out of your control.

In your imagination, put on the glasses of your soul to help you see your soul more clearly and ask yourself, 'What was my soul looking to experience as a result of this crisis?' Think about what your soul is trying to master from the situation.

Now say, 'I thank and appreciate all those people who contributed toward these opportunities for growth. I am a more complete person as a result of this experience. Thank you.'

Embracing wholeness

The law of gender decrees that all of life is formed on two major energies – divine masculine and divine feminine. Throughout this book we have covered various aspects of conditioning and programming and I have shared many tools that will allow you to access the truth of who you are. One of the most powerful truths that we can embrace under this principle is that we chose our parents and they are perfect, just the way they are.

In human form, our parents often get the rough end of the stick because they are involved in helping us learn painful or challenging lessons on a soul level. We blame them for most of our issues, because as children our first point of contact with divine masculine and feminine was through them, so we take their words as the words of God. If a father says to his child, 'You are stupid,' then the child will remain stupid for their entire life to prove their father right. If the mother says, 'You are good for nothing,' then it becomes a subconscious command and life will become a series of 'failures' so the mother can be right! It is a part of the process to feel the disconnection. As an Awakened being it is important to recognize that our parents gave us the best they could with the knowledge they had.

> *The way of an Awakened being isn't the way of the optimist who says the glass is half full, or the pessimist who says it's half empty. An Awakened person declares the glass is full – half of air and half of water. Just because you can't see it doesn't mean it's not there!*

Daily Practice: Healing your relationship with your parents

This is one of the most powerful processes in your Awakening because once you acknowledge that Nothing Is Missing from your parents then you will start to see the lessons that your soul received during your upbringing.

Find a peaceful space where you won't be disturbed and relax there for a few minutes, focusing on your breath.

Relax deeply and connect with yourself as a spiritual being who has many glorious layers of consciousness. Imagine that you're rising upward to what looks like a starry sky. Go up and up into the soul plane, you are fully aware about this plane and you look around and see lots of stars twinkling around you; this is your superconscious where your eternal timeline is stored.

In the distance you see a few stars that are brighter than the others and, as you move toward those brighter lights, you sense that these are the souls of your biological parents, your step-parents or your adoptive parents, whether they are living or are now in spirit. You acknowledge them by nodding and all three, four or five of you – however many parental souls you find, nod back to acknowledge you. You find yourselves flying together and you all land on a riverbank.

Feel your feet on the ground and see and hear the river flowing past. The birds are singing and the leaves on the trees are rustling. Allow your mind to just rest and your consciousness to become engaged in this process.

Imagine that the crown of your head is opening and a shaft of light is coming down from the sky, moving down your spine and filling your body with its energy. As you are filled with light you become your higher self. You become the light that you are – wise, peaceful, pure love.

In the distance you see your parents approaching and with each step they take they become more and more filled with light. Your parents walk toward you and, like you, they have become their higher selves, all wise, all loving. First, acknowledge them for showing up and allowing you to be with them. Then allow your mother to stand on your left-hand side and allow your father to stand on your right. Invite all those other souls who might not have been your parents but who have had had a major influence in your life as either a father- or a mother-figure – invite their higher selves as well.

Now, see a cord almost like an umbilical cord emanating from your belly button connecting you to your mother's side, so you see your biological mother connected with the placenta. You might also see a cord connecting you with your adoptive mother, stepmother or grandmother or any other influential mother figure.

On your right side there's a cord from your solar plexus (see page 131) connecting you to your father's solar plexus. And you might see other fatherly figures connected to you with a cord, maybe to a different chakra, maybe your root chakra at the base of your spine. This represents a major influence around your issues with money and programming around home issues. See the cord connecting you from your root chakra to their root chakra. As you see yourself you feel all these cords connecting you with these father figures and they represent all the emotional, spiritual, psychic, sexual and any other issues or programming that you have picked up from them. You are now going to invite a major healing to take place, so give yourself permission to receive this transmission.

Say, 'Please bring down healing energy to the point and time where all traumas are held between me and my father or any fatherly figure. I command that any memories of shock or previous actions be absorbed from my cellular memory, the neuron system, the limbic system and anywhere else it is held. I invite you to experience this healing in your cellular memory.'

Imagine a light is entering your cells and command the reabsorption of any negative imprints from your father's stresses, his attitudes, his beliefs, his fears, his traumas, his judgments that have influenced your career, money, relationships or your health.

Say, 'Please reabsorb all shocks from my body's consciousness. Please reabsorb all ancestral imprints of shock and trauma. I command that all scars, physical, energetical, emotional, mental or spiritual, that have been created from my father please be removed. Please clear the Akashic and soul records. I command a genetic memory to go back to the time before the trauma was held. I command that all negative emotions – anger, despair, grief, anguish, terror, guilt, shame, hopelessness, rejection, abandonment, mistrust, sadness, greed, unworthiness – be balanced with the energy of love. I invite all my own soul fragments into my cellular memory.'

Now, see the cords between you and your father start to dissolve. Turn your attention to your father and say to him, 'Thank you so much for showing up in my life and agreeing to teach me all these lessons. I let go of any vows, any contracts, any pacts, any agreements, any promises, any decisions that I made to myself or that I made to you or any of the fatherly figures who stop me from being in this energy of the divine masculine. I declare them all complete and I ask God in his expression of divine masculine to enter the right-hand side of my body.'

Imagine a shaft of energy opening at the top of your head on the right-hand side of your body and this beautiful energy entering your body, every cell, every nerve just bathing in this beautiful energy, just allowing you to transcend any judgments, any beliefs, any fears, any unworthiness that you have been accumulating in your body regarding power – just release it.

Now turn your attention to the left-hand side of your body. Look at your mother, your biological mother and all the other major mothering influences you have experienced. Say, 'Please bring down the healing energies to the points and times where the trauma is held in my body's consciousness. I command the reabsorption of any negative imprints from her stresses, attitudes, beliefs, fears and judgments that I have picked up. Please reabsorb all shock from the body's consciousness, please reabsorb all ancestral programming that has influenced my relationships with men, money, health and home. I release them all. I command that all shock on the soul level be reabsorbed and that my soul may be grounded back to perfection. I command that all of my mother's blocked negative emotions – fear, anger, despair, grief, anguish, terror, guilt, shame, hopelessness, rejection, abandonment, mistrust, unworthiness – be balanced with the energy of pure love. I command all the muscular and memory systems be regenerated and rejuvenated back to perfection. I command that the etheric fields to be repaired back to perfection. Please clear the contracts between me and mother and her mother. Please remove any scarring, physical, mental, emotional and spiritual. I welcome back all my soul fragments.'

Now, imagine the cords between you and your mother dissolving, that placenta that represents any unemotional, any emotional unresolved patterns. You say to your mother and all the major mothering influences in your life, 'With love I let go of any vows, any contracts, any agreements, any promises that I made to you or you made to me that stop me from being in a loving relationship with myself and the rest of the world. Let me be in optimum health and clear anything that stops me from being comfortable in my own skin or from being seen. I release any guilt, shame, revenge, punishment, repression, anger and resentment that you have given me against men, women, society, money, home, in-laws, siblings and children and I declare them all complete. I lovingly set you free.'

As you say these words you can see the cords are now dissolving. Ask the Universe to help you embrace the divine feminine goddess and imagine a shaft of energy opening at the top of your head on the left-hand side of your body. Every nerve, every fibre and every cell in your body is bathed in this beautiful energy, transcending any beliefs, judgments, fears, programming and decisions that you have made that stop you from activating your intuition.

Allow it all to be transcended so you can now marry the divine masculine and divine feminine in your body. Feel the energy merging from both sides of your body, creating a beautiful marriage between the divine masculine and divine feminine in your space. You have let go of your representation of god and goddess, of your mum and your dad, and you know that they are spiritual beings having a human experience just as are you.

You are releasing their reality from your space and enjoying this beautiful bathing of masculine and feminine. Breathe in and breathe out any resistance. Breathe in and breathe out once more and then when you're ready you can slowly and gradually come back into the room, into your body. Gently pat your legs and your arms and return to your day.

The keys to living the eighth principle

The following keys will assist you in activating the eighth principle, Nothing Is Missing, in your day-to-day life.

Responsibility
Responsibility just means activating your ability to respond to a situation. Life is made up of choices and decisions, which always bring responsibility with them. As we discovered in the seventh principle, It Takes One To See One, every action leads to a reaction, every cause has its consequences. The more you acknowledge and become answerable for your choices, the more empowered you will feel.

Patience
Sometimes the answers or the awareness won't come to you straight away. You might not understand the lesson you need to learn instantly. Everything happens in its own good time and having patience with your own lessons will allow them to integrate with divine timing.

Appreciation
Counting what you have in life and shifting your focus from lack to abundance through appreciation works like magic in embracing this principle.

Faith
This is one of the most important keys in Nothing Is Missing! Having faith that the Universe has your back, whatever life throws at you, will help you become closer to who you are.

Taking charge of your destiny

It may be tempting to think that because everything is perfect as it is you won't have to put any energy into growing or changing. Your ego probably got excited when it first read about this truth because, hey, if everything is already perfect, well why make an effort? You don't have to change but if you want to get back to the divine Source of all love then you will need to. As you are a powerful co-creator of your life you can choose the experiences you want to master on this earth plane. You can decide to go toward abundance, love, health, joy or whatever you want, but you still have work to do! Maybe you decided that part of your soul purpose, part of your destiny, is to deal with the fear of change, to be decisive and to act!

ACTIVATING THE EIGHTH PRINCIPLE: NOTHING IS MISSING

In the eighth step of the Awakening journey, Nothing Is Missing, we put everything that has ever happened in any of our timelines into perspective. When you can truly own the principle that everything is working to perfection, then you will let go of the need to hold on to resentment, anger, guilt, judgment or any other emotion that is stopping you from making the most of life. When you look back in hindsight, knowing that every decision you made was the right one at the time (otherwise you wouldn't have made it), you will realize that you had everything you needed all along.

In the ninth principle, Growth Is Inevitable, you'll discover what it means to live as an Awakened being and how you'll experience growth in all your relationships as the Wheel of Life turns.

Divine Magic Statement

I am who I am. I am where I am.

THE NINTH PRINCIPLE

Growth Is Inevitable

'You can cut all the flowers but you can't keep spring from coming.'

Pablo Neruda

The truth of the ninth principle is that we can't prevent growth, we are part of the ebb and flow of life and change is part of our experience. Activating this truth means we accept every single event that has happened to us and understand that all future events beckon us to evolve. Change brings pain but by consciously integrating all our experiences in our current, ancestral and eternal timelines we bring life into balance and live as an Awakened being. Using the Nine Principles of Awakening we rise above blame, make our own choices and take charge of our own actions so that we can live in truth and fulfil our purpose on the earth and soul planes. When we do this we, ultimately, experience the unconditional love that dissolves all separation and become an expression of the divine – the Source of all creation.

Change is pain

The reason you chose the Awakening and followed it here is because you already resonate with the truth, Growth Is Inevitable. On some level you knew we would always meet here. When we choose to undertake the journey of Awakening and evolve it is usually because the pain of holding on to what we have becomes greater than the pain brought by change; this is the catalyst for us to take action. Whenever something happens to us that doesn't fit with the way we feel the world ought to be we encounter change. The irony is that life is change; enduring change is the name of the game. As the Greek philosopher Heraclitus said, 'You cannot step twice into the same river.' Instead of viewing Growth as Inevitable as a natural part of life, most of us try to avoid it at all costs.

THE BROTHERS

Two seeds were talking together in the rich earth where they had been sown by a farmer. 'This is so exciting!' exclaimed one. 'We're going to grow into plants! Our roots will wriggle into the earth and draw up all the goodness there. Our delicate green seedlings will push up into the sunlight and people will smile to know that spring is on its way. Rain will fall on us and sunshine too, and we will grow strong.'

His brother was scared. 'Creatures live down there that will nip off our roots. And what lies above the surface? Perhaps a great rock will crush us as we try to push up. Even if we do make it to the surface, we may be trampled by animals or the farmer's boots. And if we ever grow, our leaves will be eaten by snails and slugs. I'm staying here, where it's safe.' The first seed grew into a fine, strong plant, but his brother did nothing. And a little later a bird scratching in the earth uncovered the seed – and ate it!

Change is a fundamental law of nature. A flower's growth cycle is obvious to us as it sprouts, buds, blossoms and fades away in its short lifespan. Mighty mountains, deserts, seas and planets change over a much longer timeframe, taking millions of years, outside of our human perception. Nature is in a state of constant change. Summer gives way to fall, fall gives way to winter, winter to spring, and spring to summer. Like everything else in nature, our lives constantly undergo change and we struggle and suffer if we deny its power.

> *Nothing stays still. Life is in constant motion from a molecular to a planetary level and we transform right along with it. The Universe moves in a perpetual surging dance. The very air you breathe in changes when it comes out again!*

But if the nature of life is change, then why does it cause us so much fear and unhappiness? Why do we resist it so deeply and struggle against it so desperately when we know that constant adaptation and modification create the momentum and energy that keeps us going? It is because our ego wants to control our life.

The illusion of control

Our conscious perception of reality is limited. If we understood the real nature of the Universe it would stop us from learning and growing. Your ego wants you to believe that you know all the answers and that your actions control your world. But, of course, nature's cycle of life and death cannot be influenced by anyone or anything. Your ego isn't very happy about that. In fact, it's terrified because in order for you to feel important, you need to believe that your spark of life is the brightest one of all!

Our ego is responsible for our struggle to get to the top of our game. But when you recognize the truth of who you really are – that your true nature is an eternal flame, not a spark, then your ego will finally understand the illusion it has been clinging to. We are all one. The journey you have been on throughout the Awakening has taught you to listen to what's in your heart and soul rather than giving in to your ego's temporary highs. When you experience the truth your ego stops banging its head against the wall and the true nature of pain is revealed.

Pain's purpose

The reality of human behaviour is that only two things move people to act: pain or pleasure. Physical pain reminds us of the inevitable – that our body won't last forever. Pain is a signal that our body sends to our brain to take action to stop the uncomfortable feeling. Pain tells us we need to change something. Humankind would not have lasted very long if we didn't react to pain. The first time you scalded yourself on the oven might have finished you off! The body is fragile and pain reminds us that we need to look after it if we want to thrive.

Emotional pain does the same job: uncomfortable feelings alert us to something that needs to change. When we ignore those signals for long periods we become used to the distress and accept the pain as part of life. The truth is that it is only when you are feeling deeply uncomfortable, severely unhappy or unfulfilled in your current situation that you are likely to expand your comfort zone and start searching for a different way to relieve your pain. We think that if we resist unwanted situations for long enough then they will disappear without our intervention. But by resisting change, our pain does not go anywhere – it just makes us suffer more.

Our ego will do whatever it can to create feelings of safety, security and a sense of mastery over the external world. Your human mind would much prefer if everything remained the same because that's the only way it feels secure. Consciously, you want a better job, to live in a nicer area, to stick to a healthier lifestyle or be in a more loving relationship, but if you let the fear of change in you will remain in exactly the same situation. We fear what we don't know, even if what we don't know could be infinitely better than what we already have. We long for change in life but find any amount of excuses not to make our dreams come true. Then we become so comfortable with our discomfort that it becomes normal. It is usually not until something becomes unbearable in our lives that we are forced to make a move, when we should have taken action a long time ago.

FREDDIE THE FROG

Freddie hopped into a pot of water and found that he couldn't easily get out again. The water was delightfully warm so he swam about enjoying himself, assuming that someone would be along shortly to help him out. Gradually the water became warmer and warmer and the experience was not so pleasant. It was really quite hot now. He knew he could probably get out in one gigantic leap but the sides of the pot were high and Freddie could not see what was beyond them. He was scared that he might fall and hurt himself. He focused on trying to cope with the heat.

Freddie was now in real pain but he was still scared of making the leap. He needed all his energy just to stay alive and he was very tired. Then the water began to boil. Freddie understood at last that he was in terrible trouble and needed to escape right now. He summoned all his energy to jump to freedom, but he could barely rise above the surface of the water. All Freddie's strength had drained away in his struggle to

> adapt to the deteriorating situation and now he could not help himself. And that, unfortunately, was the end of Freddie.

You might think the boiling water killed Freddie but the thing that caused Freddie's death was timing! What pot do you need to jump out of before you don't have the time or the energy? We don't always notice the water getting hotter until it's too late. Change is not always perceptible to us – we don't notice ourselves changing until we see physical signs of aging in our bodies. We wake up one day and look at ourselves in the mirror and think where did the last 20 years go?

BETTER THE DEVIL YOU KNOW

Sylvia was in a toxic relationship with her husband, Julian, for 12 years. Things were good when they were first married, but after a year Sylvia got pregnant with their first and only child, Matthew. The pregnancy was unplanned and Julian couldn't cope with the responsibility and the changes that having a baby entailed. He vanished for four months, leaving Sylvia to cope with their newborn.

Sylvia was miserable and angry, but kept giving Julian the benefit of the doubt. Julian continued to abandon them frequently in the years to come, especially when times got tough and they needed him the most. When Matthew was four, Julian moved out of their house and was only in touch occasionally, even though their son was diagnosed with type-1 diabetes and Sylvia desperately needed his support. Sylvia kept hoping Julian would change but he seemed to struggle with making any commitment to his wife and child.

Julian was in and out of Sylvia and Matthew's life for 12 years and when she came to see me she was ready to separate from him but admitted part of her was still clinging on to the idea that things would get better; that her marriage could still work. I asked what she thought she was getting out of the relationship, what it was that she was so scared of changing.

She said, 'I don't think I want to admit that I was wrong. It seems that if I end it now I have lost almost 15 years of my life because I didn't want to face up to it not being a great situation. I wanted to believe that on some level he really loved us both, but now I see that even if that is true, it's not enough'

I heard from Sylvia a year later. She told me that after she divorced Julian she felt lighter. Instead of reacting maliciously toward her, Julian accepted the divorce and now sees Matthew more regularly and seems to have taken more responsibility for his son as he understands Sylvia really means business. It seems that by taking responsibility for the changes, Sylvia made Julian face up to his own issues, too.

Accepting the inevitable

New beginnings are often disguised as painful endings. When compared with the evolution of the natural world, our human lifespan is as short as a dragonfly's. We think that our

40-year-old parents are as ancient as the hills when we are teenagers, and when we're 40 we only just begin to appreciate how little time we have left! The universal law of change perpetually operates throughout the earth plane as we observe its transformations, the cycles of life and death.

Inevitably, we must accept that our body and those of everyone we love will face the final change – death.

Loss teaches us a great many lessons – often the most profound in our lives. Only when we lose something or someone we truly care about do we really appreciate what it is to love or cherish the things in our lives that we often take for granted. Loss also makes us appreciate the ever-present 'now' because what we feel we have lost is now in the past, and we feel we can never return to that place. But our memories and experiences of that situation, place or person have formed who we are today.

Grief changes our philosophy of life because change is forced upon us, often in a way that we are unable to prepare for. Dealing with such overwhelming emotions can make us grow, even if we feel frozen to the spot. Our empathy with others who are coping with the same experience strengthens our bonds with some people in our life, or makes us see that our relationships with certain others don't have enough room for us both to grow. We feel at our most vulnerable, yet in other ways our deep appreciation for the reality of the cycle of life and death make us much stronger.

Understanding and experiencing what death is really about is a powerful lesson in transformation.

However, many of us avoid dealing with the inevitability that death and grief brings. But when we don't accept it, it can show up in different areas of our lives without us even knowing. As the following story demonstrates, I have many clients who hold on to their departed loved ones, which manifests as weight concerns, emotional pain or even financial limitations, rather than accept that death and life are part of the cycle of life.

HOLDING ON

At one of my live Awakening events, when I was talking about weight issues, I asked the audience if anyone wanted to join me on stage and was willing to address their challenges surrounding being overweight. Galena volunteered and as soon as she came up on stage I felt a presence with her. I asked her, 'Has someone passed away recently?' she started crying in response. Even though her brother had died a couple of years before, she missed him incredibly and felt that after her brother's death she had lost her 'protection' from the world. She felt vulnerable and lacked confidence since he had died. We went through the bereavement process (given overleaf) together and she said 'goodbye' to her brother.

Later she told me she had dropped a dress size within a week without changing her diet. As she felt it so difficult to let go of her brother, she had been 'holding on' to him by 'holding on' to the extra weight around her body which subconsciously also represented her need for 'protection'.

As an Awakened being, we accept the truth of the fifth principle that Energy is Everything and that energy cannot be destroyed – it just changes form. So when we lose loved ones the grieving process is part of the process of life and can no more be denied than each day turning to night.

Daily Practice: Saying goodbye

The following process can help you make peace with your loved ones who are no longer in this physical reality.

Breathe in and out a few times to help you become calm and focused. Feel fully present in your body.

Now, imagine that you are breathing in a pure white light that is shifting you into a higher and higher state of consciousness. Just keep breathing. The light you're breathing in is allowing you to become your higher self in a different dimension. You're enjoying this experience of becoming your wiser, higher self.

Eventually, as you shift your state of consciousness, a fine silvery mist surrounds you. As the mist clears you become aware that you are in a mystical place. This is a sacred space and an ascended master greets you – this could be Jesus, Buddha, Saint Michael, Merlin or any other guide that your vibration is willing to receive. The master leads you to a sacred garden. It is a beautiful place that feels different to any you have been to before.

As you walk through that space you know that you haven't visited this place before. You feel a sense of knowingness, that this is another realm. As you walk your heart starts beating faster with excitement because you know something special is about to happen. You find yourself in front of a gate and on the other side of that gate is a mist. You know that someone special or some special being is about to visit you. When your ascended master nods, the mist dissipates and you see your loved one who is now in spirit. Connect with the energy of your loved one.

The gate represents the difference between you in this realm and them in the other realm but you can still see, feel and hear their presence. If you miss them, tell them. If they're asking for forgiveness, forgive them. This is your time to heal any grudges, regrets or guilt that your cellular memory has been holding onto.

As soon as your message is understood they will begin to fade away. They have to carry on their journey and you have to lovingly let them be.

When they are gone and you feel calm, say this completion prayer, 'With love, I let go of any vows, any contracts, any pacts, any agreements, any promises, any decisions that I made to you or to myself that stop me from living my life on the earth plane or that prevent me from being at ease in my own body. I declare them all complete.

'I lovingly release any psychic cords, sexual cords, karmic cords, relational cords, paternal cords, maternal cords, religious cords or any other cords that keeps us attached, I lovingly dissolve them. Thank you for showing up in my reality.'

Now it's time to be open to receiving the love your lost person wants you to feel. They are so grateful and appreciative that you have connected with them.

Bid them a final goodbye and send them more love. Then slowly and gradually begin to come back into your body, taking your time, opening your eyes into this dimension.

Experiencing growth

When you start to use this principle you must remind yourself that the pain you're in is worse than the pain of the change itself. For example, the fear that you won't be able to make enough money to pay your bills is far worse than what will happen if you take steps toward getting a new job or asking for better pay. The fear comes from a primitive part of you that thinks change brings endings. But if you can get yourself used to making changes, small to begin with then building up to more profound ones, you'll begin to trust yourself more and will soon realize that change is something you can survive – and even thrive on.

> *Slowly coax yourself out of the subconscious cave,*
> *into the light of day.*

Keep reminding yourself that the Universe has your back by keeping your Awareness journal so you can keep track of how your life is expanding. Write down your intentions and plan how to make your dreams become a reality. Read about inspiring people who transformed their situations to remind you of what you are capable of too.

Remember, too, that you become the people you surround yourself with, so keep in regular touch with people who are in alignment with your Awakening journey. Many times all that is required from the people around us is these magical words, 'I believe in you'. Tell the people you love that you believe in their ability to create the life they desire and watch as this is mirrored back into your own situation.

Your faith in the Universe's ultimate plan will allow you to embrace the pain of change and keep you on the right track. Pain is a part of the process but suffering is optional – it is an emotional response to an event and a natural process of change.

> *Whether you're dealing with fear, resistance or pain,*
> *each of those challenging emotions is showing you*
> *the way forward. It's the judgments you create around*
> *those experiences that will create more suffering.*

The more you apply this principle to your life, the more skilled and experienced you'll become at handling life's curveballs. You will either grow kicking and screaming or you'll let go – either way you are growing!

Decisions, decisions

Every day we make a multitude of choices that impact our life. Some of these choices are minor and will only influence the next few minutes, hours or days, while others will completely change the direction in which we're headed.

Some choices are easy to make. Some are more challenging. Even though your heart knows the answer, your mind usually gets in the way.

Daily Practice: Making decisions

This process will enable your heart's choice to shine through as you learn to tap into the energy of the future result of that decision without actually having to make the decision itself.

Close your eyes and take few deep breaths to become fully present in your body.

Once you feel relaxed, rapidly and consciously imagine yourself standing in a hallway.

In front of you are three wooden doors. Each door has a sign on the front of it: 'Decision A', 'Decision B', and 'Decision C', representing three possible outcomes of the decision you have to make. Know now that 'Decision C' is always the best possible outcome from the Universe.

Breathe deeply then approach and open Door A. Walk through the door, knowing that by entering you are choosing to make Decision A. Close the door behind you, becoming fully present in the room that is behind Door A. Perceive how your life has turned out as a result of taking that decision. See, hear, feel and touch whatever is in the room. Use all your five senses to engage in the energy and when you feel you have got an experience of what the outcome of making Decision A would be like, leave the room, closing the door behind you.

Then, taking a deep breathe again, repeat the process by going through Door B. Perceive how your life has turned out as a result of making that decision. See, hear, feel and touch whatever is in the room. Use all your five senses to engage in the energy and when you feel you have got an experience of what the outcome of making Decision B would be like, leave the room, closing the door behind you.

Lastly, breathe deeply again and open Door C. Remember, you have asked the Universe to show you the best possible outcome behind Door C so enter the room and experience exactly what this is in the same way as above. See what the Universe holds and perceive the information that comes to you.

Levels of growth

Growth occurs on four levels: physical, mental, emotional and spiritual, and there is an intrinsic relationship between them as they are part of the Wheel of Life that I described earlier (see page 43). Growth in one area will affect growth in the next. Using the following Daily Practice will help keep you open to change and keep you flowing with life as the wheel turns.

Daily Practice: Wheel of Life

Physical growth
One of the kindest things you can do for your physical growth is to bless the food you eat. Food is a form of energy and it has transformational effects on our physical wellbeing. Here's how to reprogram the energy

of the food you eat to allow optimum nutrition on a spiritual level.

Before you eat your food say, 'I bless all of this food and everyone who has contributed toward bringing this food to my table. Please allow me to reprogram the cellular memory of this food to my optimum health. Allow any part of the food that does not serve me to pass through and all that does to give me optimum health, vitality and energy. Thank you.' And now, enjoy your food.

Mental growth

We can use the great capacity of our minds to search for answers that will change our perspective and lead to growth and expansion. Try asking these quality questions when you feel stuck:

- What is great about this problem?
- How does it get even better than this?
- What am I willing to do to make this the way I want it?
- What am I willing to give up to make this the way I want it?

Emotional growth

As human beings, we like to hold on to everything, including emotions that no longer serve us. This process is one of the most powerful and profound processes to let go of all those people in the past who no longer serve you in the present.

Close your eyes and take few deep breaths in to become fully present in your body.

Now, choose a person you want to work on, ideally this should be someone you feel you need to let go of.

Notice which part of your body responds when you think about that person to discover where the energetic charge around that person is located in the specific part of your body.

Imagine in your mind's eye that all that energy is leaving your body and coming outside of you to form an image of that person in front of you. Know that it is safe for you to be in front of that person.

Repeat these words aloud, 'I love you. I am sorry that we have got to this stage. Please forgive me, I forgive you, we are both free. I choose to let go of your energy from my space and I retrieve all my energy from yours. Thank you.'

Repeat these words three times and notice how it feels after saying it a few times. Take few deep breaths in while integrating.

Drink a glass of water and return to enjoy being you.

Spiritual growth

From the fifth principle, Energy Is Everything, we know that we are an expression of the Source and we are here to experience this earth plane like the Source. One of the best ways to develop the connection with this God-self is to meditate on connecting with your higher self.

Close your eyes and take a few deep breaths to become fully present in your body . . . Now, pick a symbol for your higher self; this could be a diamond, a flower, a waterfall or anything that you feel represents clarity, wisdom or power.

Say, 'Hello' to your higher self and feel the love, peace and joy that is present within your higher being. Now, imagine you are receiving an energetic transmission from your higher self that contains wisdom, love and peace.

Doing this process every day for a few minutes will also open up your inner vision and help you to be able to perceive the invisible energies on the earth plane.

Identity crisis

Inner growth can make you question who you are. As you grow, your identity keeps changing. The difficulty arises when you try to align yourself with an outdated identity. This usually happens when we are afraid to make other people uncomfortable with our growth. In my experience, criticism and judgment from people around us is usually a sign that we are growing.

The reason for this is that our friends or loved ones might feel that in changing we may also alter our values or our opinions of them. For example, if you decide to take better care of your health and give up your Friday night drinking sessions after work, your drinking buddies may feel you've changed in a way they're not happy with, or may think your ideas about who they are have changed and it could make them uncomfortable. And if your Friday night out is a big part of your identify, then you will need something that's just as fulfilling to replace that with.

The same idea applies if, for example, you decide you no longer want to be your sister's sounding board about her stressful job or your friend's shoulder to lean on when he needs a loan.

Daily Practice: Releasing roles

The following practice can help you and others in your life come to terms with the loss of your old way of being and accept you without judgment.

Simply write your name in the middle of a piece of paper then write all of the roles you can possibly think of that you play in life. Your list might include roles such as friend, teacher, sister, brother, parent, lover, caregiver, cleaner, rescuer, financier, your job role, etc.

Now ask yourself these quality questions and take a note of your answers in your Awakening journal:

- How many of these roles do you enjoy playing?

- How many feel like chores and don't feel light and expansive when you think about them?

Close your eyes and drop your awareness all the way into the part of yourself that has access to wisdom, power and perception.

Ask yourself, 'Where do I most feel this role in my body?'

Allow that energy to leave your body and stand in front of you. Say, 'I love you. I am sorry, please forgive me. I forgive you. We are both free. I release all this energy from all levels, dimensions and timelines. Higher levels please take charge and replace it with my true energy. Thank you.'

Taking inspired action

One of the secrets to a happy life is not to get out of your comfort zone, but to expand it. If something is working for you, why change it? But if you know it needs working on, then you must at least try to shift it.

If the fear of change is still holding you back from making a particular move, try doing something that is completely different from your usual activities. Doing something exciting or adventurous, which you wouldn't ordinarily dream of, can teach you that just because something is new, shouldn't make it frightening. Making the unknown known could be as simple as taking a new route to work or trying your hand at skydiving – it all depends on your current level of comfort.

> For some people, jumping out of a plane from 10,000 feet is utter craziness. For me, it was an act of surrendering into divinity and expanding my comfort zone.

The essence of the principle that Growth Is Inevitable is in taking responsibility for your life and in learning to embrace change. Change is wonderful! Think of all the things you would like to try but have not had the chance or the courage to try. Ask yourself these quality questions:

- What is it about life that you really enjoy?
- Would you like to see the pyramids or glaciers?
- Have you always wanted to sing on stage or give a giraffe a hug?
- Do you want to write a book or sing in a choir or join a theatre group but have never had time?

Making a list of the things you would really like to see or do before your time is up will remind you that there's a whole world of experiences that you could be part of if you wanted to be. The secret is to embrace all change, and know that it will help you to continuing growing.

THE STREAM

A stream once went exploring through the land. It burbled happily through the plains and mountains, making its way with no trouble around obstacles such as pebbles and rocks. Then it encountered the desert. Sand was a problem that the stream had not faced before. Whenever it tried to continue through the sands, it lost itself – the water just slipped away. Each attempt to proceed was met with failure. 'Does my story end here?' asked the stream.

A wise voice was borne on the wind, 'You will have to change if you want to cross the desert. To continue

---

on your path you must lose your old self and find a new one.'

'But how can that be?' asked the stream. 'If I lose myself I will no longer exist.'

'Quite the opposite,' said the voice. 'In losing what you think you are, you will grow beyond your former limitations and become more than ever before.'

The stream surrendered to its destiny and allowed its waters to evaporate in the burning heat of the sun. In cloud form the stream journeyed across the vast desert. At last, in a great rainstorm, its waters descended to the earth once more and so the stream continued on its path around the world.

The art of surrender

According to the Greek philosopher Aristotle there is always a reason for everything that happens. Painful circumstances in your life are a catalyst to help you to transcend the Veil of Amnesia and reconnect with your soul's purpose. They are not meant to be permanent, and you can always choose to direct your energy toward healing and growth, rather than feeling sorry for yourself over the perceived judgment of these circumstances.

Life has always gone on. Nothing is ever lost or wasted; not time, not love, not energy and not your decisions and choices, even when they lead to painful circumstances. Pain is meant to wake us up to who we are. As CS Lewis said, 'Pain insists upon being attended to. God whispers to us in our pleasures, speaks in our consciences, but shouts in our pains. It is his megaphone to rouse a deaf world.'

250

THE RING

Once upon a time a king struggled continually between ecstasy and despair. He would become emotional at the smallest things, but any joy he felt faded as quickly as it had arisen.

One day the king was in a dark mood and he decided to try to find a solution for his emotional turmoil. He summoned a famous sage to court. When the sage appeared, the king said, 'You have a reputation as an enlightened man. I, too, want equanimity and serenity in my life. If you can help me achieve inner peace I will pay you whatever you desire.'

'I may be able to help you,' said the sage, 'but do not offer payment. Your entire kingdom would not be enough. Instead, I will give this wisdom to you freely, as a gift, if you will honour it.'

The king promised to behave as the sage requested, and the sage departed. When he returned some time later he offered the king a beautiful jade box. Inside the box the king found a plain gold ring carved with the words, 'This, too, shall pass.' The king questioned the sage eagerly about the ring's meaning.

'Wear this ring,' said the sage, 'and look at it whenever you feel joy or despair arising in you as a response to some event. You will remember then that everything must pass, and by doing this you will always be at peace.'

The possibilities for growth are endless once you recognize that you have the power to choose how you want to feel and live. The secret to happiness is not to cling to anything or anyone too tightly but to appreciate that everything changes with time.

ACTIVATING THE NINTH PRINCIPLE: GROWTH IS INEVITABLE

In the ninth and final step of the Awakening journey, Growth Is Inevitable, we discover how the end of the journey is always the beginning. Pain always follows huge energetic shifts. In order to embrace growth and transcend your suffering, you have to go against your instincts to hold on and give yourself over to what is happening. In surrendering you allow yourself to let go of any expectations you have and accept whatever life is truly presenting to you in that moment.

Once you let go of how you can fix, transform or mend what is happening, you automatically give way for life to flow. It's like hitting ice when driving. Most people have an impulse to steer away, but steering into the skid puts us more in control. This is the secret to breaking free. Embracing the ninth principle we realize that the Awakening is not an event but a way of being and in every moment of the journey we are growing.

Divine Magic Statement

All of my needs and desires are fulfilled by the Divine Grace.

Living An Awakened Life

Welcome to the Land of Awakening. Now that you understand the truths of the Awakening you will become the living embodiment of what it is to live an Awakened life. Even as an Awakened being you will still experience the ups and downs of living on the earth plane, but you now have the tools to minimize the contrast between good, bad, right, wrong, happiness and sadness, and can embrace everything as a learning experience for your soul. By embodying the power and wisdom of the Nine Principles of Awakening you will be able to identify, accept and release any old programming that is no longer working for you. After all, just like the dragonfly in the story below, our challenges are all part of our soul's destiny to evolve.

THE DRAGONFLY

Some nymphs once lived a happy life in a quiet pool. Their days were spent swimming in the muddy water and eating tadpoles, and no one bothered them. They had only one trouble: every so often, one of the nymphs would climb a reed, out of the water, never to be seen again. The nymphs understood that this meant the death of their comrade.

One day a certain water nymph felt that he must climb the reed. There was no resisting the urge, but as he climbed he decided that he was not going to

---

abandon his friends as so many other nymphs had done before. He would certainly go back.

The nymph was out of the water now and the strange warmth of the sun was making him sleepy. He couldn't resist lying down, just for a moment. The reed was very comfortable and soon the nymph was fast asleep.

When he woke up he felt completely different. Somehow, he just knew he could fly. And so he did! As he swooped and soared he saw that his old nymph body had been replaced by an amazing new one, with huge gauzy wings. He had not died. He had become a dragonfly!

From his new viewpoint he saw that the world was much larger than he had ever suspected. He had not forgotten his friends but he knew that his new body would not allow him to return to share the good news with them. But he also knew that they, too, were destined to follow him. So he raised his wings and flew into the Land of Awakening.

Daily Practice creates change

Using the Daily Practices will cause a profound shift in your everyday life. If you do feel stuck, go back and activate the energy of the Awakening principle that most applies to your situation. The exercises below work in tandem with the healing processes and Divine Magic Statement associated with each of the Nine Principles of Awakening. Keep in mind that your real problem is not that you are experiencing a problem, but that you are staying in the 'problem zone' and not doing anything about it. I love Winston Churchill's take on this, 'If you are going through hell, keep going.'

Daily Practice: Six rituals

Practised daily these six rituals can help you maintain your Awakening journey in the days, months and years to come. They should be practised in sequence and each should take five minutes.

1 Five-minute conversation

Pick a journal and start writing as if you are talking to the Universe. Whatever comes into your mind, write it down. The words don't even have to make sense for this to open up channels of communication with the Universe.

2 Five-minute silence

Empty your mind and focus on nothingness. Allow your mind to drift and stay focused on the present moment.

3 Five-minute resolution

Make a list of all those people you find challenging. Go through each person and imagine them in your mind's eye. To each person, say 'I am sorry. I forgive you and am forgiven, we are both free. Thank you.'

4 Five-minute appreciation

Write down all the things you appreciate in your life. Whatever comes to your mind, just keep writing and don't stop until the five minutes is up.

5 Five-minute visualization

Imagine light entering your day and giving you the best possible day . . . week . . . month . . . year . . . life . . . Everything you do is filled with light.

6 Five-minute manifestation

Take an aspect that you want to manifest in your life – for example, more clients, a new relationship, a house, a car, a family, etc. Now, hold the intention and imagine that you're in a courtyard. This is a special place of manifestation in the inner planes. Here, you are met by beings of light who are responsible for bringing the thought form into your reality. They circle around you, radiating love, peace, harmony and joy. Express your intention for your manifestation and imagine a matrix of light coming out of you and entering your home or workplace and going to all those energies that will contribute toward manifesting the reality. Imagine now that it has already happened and you are living that newly manifested reality. Feel the feelings of receiving in your body. Light is entering your body, updating your DNA with new space, energy and consciousness. You have received what you asked for with ease and grace.

Daily Practice: Throughout each day

Cleanse

When we sleep and go into a dream state our soul travels to other dimensions where we might pick up or absorb different emotions or ideas. It's important to have an energy shower, to clear any energy from your dream state at the start of each new day. To activate an energy shower imagine that the water of your actual shower is washing away any residual energies or emotions that may have become attracted to you in your sleep. Imagine the water to be a multi-coloured, energetic force, washing any unwanted emotions, thoughts or energy down the plughole.

Set your intention

The best way to set the tone of the day is by activating the first principle and Ask Quality Questions:

- What contribution can I make to have a [name the type of energy you want to integrate] day?
- What space can I be in to allow [name the type of energy] to show up in my life?

Clear

Spend few minutes clearing any emotions or energy that are not serving you by using the ABC process (see page 37).

Appreciate

In your Awakening journal, write down ten things you currently appreciate about your life. Or write down what you would like to manifest into your life. For example, if you desire a partner, a job or a new home write, 'I thank and appreciate my perfect partner/job/home for showing up in my reality with ease and grace.'

Declare

Before you sleep, say this: 'I declare this day complete. Allow all the lessons from the day to be integrated with ease and grace. I thank and appreciate all those people who contributed toward my journey of Awakening today. I lovingly release all of them from my energy and replace them with my true essence. Thank you.'

Daily Practice: Four steps to manifesting your dream

The energy contained in your aura is the stuff of life, the vibrational force field that everything is made from. The following process will help you harness the same unseen energy to help you manifest your dreams on to the earth plane.

1 Write down your intention

What do you want to manifest at this point? Think about what you really want to come into your life and write it down in your Awakening journal. It's usually good to keep the intentions you want to manifest to yourself because other people's thoughts or opinions about what you want to achieve could cause some interference.

For example, if I told my friend I wanted to manifest a wonderful relationship and she doesn't want that for me because she thinks I'll have less time for her, her thoughts could cause some interference. It might even be a completely subconscious thought, but it may still affect what I am trying to do. Keep your intentions to yourself and the Universe.

2 Clear the undercurrent

You now need to make sure there is no interference or undercurrent muddying your intention. Just relax and focus on the following clearing process.

Focus on your breathing and imagine there is a wonderful garden in front of you. It is a special healing place with springy green grass beneath your feet. You are safe here. Use all your senses to experience the garden. You come to a magnificent oak tree and rest your back on its trunk. You are being warmed by the sun's rays and can see a cloud coming toward you. This cloud is going to cleanse you of any fears or anxiety you have about manifesting your dream. It's getting darker and has crossed in front of the sun.

Now, imagine all the blocks that are holding you back from manifesting your dream – your fear and anxiety, guilt and anger – being sucked out of your body toward the cloud, making it darker and heavier. Imagine the fear of judgment and other people's fears and agendas leaving you in peace. Now, release your subconscious beliefs, apathy, anguish and terror, just let them drain away into the cloud . . . Now, watch the cloud moving away from you and evaporating until there is nothing left but the warm sun on your face, infusing you with its light and leaving you with a raised, cleaned vibration. Breathe in and breathe out and stay in this vibration as we move to the next step.

3 Ask for support

Standing by your tree, you begin to sense an iridescent bubble of light all around you. The bubble lifts you off the ground and carries you to a temple where there are many higher beings working together to raise human consciousness. Feel the peace, love and joy as you arrive at the temple.

Notice how beautiful the temple and the grounds are, and hear the calming undertones of chanting. Your higher self walks over to you and you feel unconditional love radiating from it toward you. Your higher self gently touches your crown chakra at the top of your head to help you awaken. Your higher self then gently touches your third eye, on the middle of your forehead, opening you inner vision and allowing you to perceive reality from a soul's point of view.

Your higher self leads you to many higher beings sitting in a circle who are sending out a broadcast of love and support to you. Feel the love and joy pouring into you. Any time you want to feel better, imagine yourself sitting in the circle receiving this broadcast and feel the warm welcome and love that is being communicated directly to you. Everyone here is sending you love and support for your intention and manifestation. Bask in the moment.

A very powerful being comes before you and asks what it is that you want to manifest on the earth plane. Express your intention. See the higher beings form a circle around you and express your intention to them. They are now with you on your journey. They are your angelic, elemental support that will help express your wish. Feel your love and connection with the earth around you and know you have the support to manifest your desires on the earth plane.

When you are ready to leave, give a cosmic hug to the higher beings and appreciate them for allowing you to experience the earth plane. Come back to your current reality, knowing you have all the support you desire. Stay with this energy as you continue to the next step.

4 Become you future self

Imagine you are whirring forward in time into your future where you have manifested your desired intention. Ask yourself,

- What date is it?
- What time is it?
- Where am I?

Use your imagination to see what life will be like when your dream comes true. Really try to see the details. For example, if it is a home, see the details of what it looks like. If it is more money, imagine seeing it in your bank account or holding it in your hands. If it is romantic love you desire, imagine the person who can give you that love.

I invite you to connect with the wisdom and consciousness of your future self by saying, 'Hello' and asking the follow questions:

- What can you teach me?
- What steps did you take to be able to manifest your dream?
- Are you are happy with the desired outcome?
- Do you have any regrets or advice?

Now, infuse your future self with your current self. Breathe in and out the wisdom of your future self into the consciousness of now. Breathe in the knowledge of your future self and breathe out your current consciousness, in with the wise future consciousness and out with your current consciousness.

Love is who you are!

In the Land of Awakening you will recognize that each and every one of us is experiencing life through love. Love doesn't recognize gender or care what country you were born in or which God you worship (if any at all) or what you do for a living. It is a love that only says, 'I love who you are.' I want to take this opportunity to say the same.

> I love, honour and acknowledge you for choosing this book and allowing me to be your guide on your Awakening journey.

May you receive the love that is infused in every chapter, every exercise and every word. I look forward to connecting with you once again when the time is right. Until we reconnect – keep allowing miracles!

With much love and appreciation,

Sidra Jafri

Further Reading

Csikszentmihalyi, Mihaly, *Flow: The Psychology of Happiness*, Rider: London, 2002 (revised and updated edition)

Edwards, Gill, *Living Magically*, Piatkus: London, 1991

Emoto, Masaru, *Messages from Water and the Universe*, Hay House: Carlsbad, CA, 2010

Gardner, Andrea, *Change Your Words, Change Your World*, Hay House: London, 2012

Hay, Louise, *You Can Heal Your Life*, Hay House: Carlsbad, CA, 1984

Jirsch, Anne, *Cosmic Energy*, Piatkus: London, 2009

Myss, Caroline, *Anatomy of the Spirit*, Bantam: London, 1997

Schein, Elyse and Bernstein, Paula, *Identical Strangers: A Memoir of Twins Separated and Reunited*, Random House: London, 2007

Awakening Events

The Awakening: Access the Courage Within
Experience Sidra's psychic and healing gifts at her one-day masterclass, which will guide you in becoming aware of and releasing your blocks in health, wealth and relationships. Throughout the day you will gain first-hand experience of the proven tools that have transformed the lives of thousands. After attending Sidra's masterclass, many people report gaining a

promotion or an increase in clients, as well as experiencing more fulfilling relationships than ever before. Sidra is the foremost expert of the new wave of personal development and she travels the world helping people awaken to their true selves. Share the space with like-minded people as you take the first steps in a life-changing journey.

Soul Spa

The six-day Soul Spa is a unique environment in which you can take time out from everyday life to discover your true soul signature and acquire the tools to live your purpose. You will:

- Heal your family matrix
- Reconnect with your truth
- Clear any karmic blocks that are keeping you stuck
- Manifest the life you desire
- Learn your unique soul destiny through numerology
- Immerse yourself in the principles of Awakening
- Recreate a blueprint of an Awakened being

Techniques covered during the Spa include journeying into the unseen realm, psychic reading and timeline reading. Sidra will help you gain a deeper understanding of your journey and equip you with the tools and know-how to release the past and overcome any future obstacles. If you are tired of the stress, the pain and the problems that have weighed you down long enough, then the Soul Spa is for you. Come and connect with your destiny. Once you are aligned with your true purpose, you will be able to move on from the difficulties in your past. You will have an amazing new sense of clarity and be able to deal with the most challenging of situations.

For further information on Awakenings, Soul Spas and other events happening in your city visit:
www.sidrajafrilive.com

WATKINS

Sharing Wisdom Since
1893

The story of Watkins Publishing dates back to March 1893, when John M. Watkins, a scholar of esotericism, overheard his friend and teacher Madame Blavatsky lamenting the fact that there was nowhere in London to buy books on mysticism, occultism or metaphysics. At that moment Watkins was born, soon to become the home of many of the leading lights of spiritual literature, including Carl Jung, Rudolf Steiner, Alice Bailey and Chögyam Trungpa.

Today our passion for vigorous questioning is still resolute. With over 350 titles on our list, Watkins Publishing reflects the development of spiritual thinking and new science over the past 120 years. We remain at the cutting edge, committed to publishing books that change lives.

DISCOVER MORE ...

Read our blog

Watch and listen to
our authors in action

Sign up to
our mailing list

JOIN IN THE CONVERSATION

 WatkinsPublishing 　　　🐦 @watkinswisdom

▶ WatkinsPublishingLtd 　　　 +watkinspublishing1893

Our books celebrate conscious, passionate, wise and happy living.
Be part of the community by visiting

www.watkinspublishing.com